MW01045081

hands-on
science
and Technology

Revised Edition

Grade 4

Senior Author
Jennifer E. Lawson

Authors
Joni Bowman
Randy Cielen
Carol Pattenden
Rita Platt

Program Consultant and Contributing Author
Sidney McKay

Program Reviewer
Jan Edwards

PORTAGE & MAIN PRESS

Winnipeg • Manitoba • Canada

Portage & Main Press acknowledges the financial support of the Government of Canada through the Book Publishing Industry Development Program (BPIDP) for our publishing activities.

The publisher would like to thank the following people for their review of the content and invaluable advice:

- Karen Boyd, Grade 3 teacher
- Jan Edwards, program consultant
- Peggy Hill, mathematics consultant
- Nancy Josephson, science and assessment consultant
- Denise MacRae, Grade 2 teacher
- Sidney McKay, Grade 6 teacher, gifted program
- Gail Ruta-Fontaine, Grade 2 teacher
- Judy Swan, Grade 1 teacher
- Barb Thomson, Grade 4 teacher

**Hands-On Science and Technology
Grade 4
Ontario, revised edition**

ISBN: 978-1-55379-179-9

Printed and bound in Canada by
The Prolific Group

Series Editors:
Leigh Hambly
Leslie Malkin
Book and Cover Design:
Relish Design Studio
Cover Photo Credits:
©iStockphoto.com/Ivan Stevanovic
©iStockphoto.com/Adam Korzekwa
©iStockphoto.com/Ina Peters
©iStockphoto.com/Craig Farish
Illustrations:
Pamela Dixon
Jess Dixon

PORTAGE & MAIN PRESS

100-318 McDermot Avenue
Winnipeg, Manitoba, Canada R3A 0A2
Toll free: 1-800-667-9673
Fax: 1-866-734-8477

Email: books@pandmpress.com
www.pandmpress.com

MIX
Paper from responsible sources
FSC® C006215

Content

▶

Introduction to
Hands-On Science and Technology

Program Introduction

Hands-On Science and Technology develops students' scientific literacy through active inquiry, problem solving, and decision making. With each activity in the program, students are encouraged to explore, investigate, and ask questions as a means of heightening their own curiosity about the world around them. Students solve problems through firsthand experiences, and by observing and examining objects within their environment. In order for young students to develop scientific literacy, concrete experience is of utmost importance—in fact, it is essential.

The Goals of the Science and Technology Program

Science and technology play a fundamental role in the lives of Canadians. In the introduction to the *Ontario Curriculum Grades 1–8 Science and Technology* (2007), the Ministry of Education states:

> During the twentieth century, science and technology played an increasingly important role in the lives of all Canadians. Science and technology underpin much of what we take for granted, including clean water, the places in which we live and work, and the ways in which we communicate with others. The impact of science and technology on our lives will continue to grow. Consequently, scientific and technological literacy for all has become the overarching objective of science and technology education throughout the world.

The Ontario Curriculum identifies three goals that form the foundation of the science and technology program. In keeping with this focus on scientific and technological literacy, these goals are the bases for the learning expectations identified in the *Hands-On Science and Technology* program.

Goal 1

To relate science and technology to society and the environment

Goal 2

To develop the skills, strategies, and habits of mind required for scientific inquiry and technological problem solving

Goal 3

To understand the basic concepts of science and technology

►

Hands-On Science and Technology Expectations

UNIT 1: HABITATS AND COMMUNITIES

Overall Expectations

- **1.0** Analyse the effects of human activities on habitats and communities

- **2.0** Investigate the interdependence of plants and animals within specific habitats and communities

- **3.0** Demonstrate an understanding of habitats and communities and the relationships among the plants and animals that live in them

Specific Expectations

- **1.1** Analyze the positive and negative impacts of human interactions with natural habitats and communities (*e.g., human dependence on natural materials*), taking different perspectives into account (*e.g., the perspectives of a housing developer, a family in need of housing, an ecologist*), and evaluate ways of minimizing the negative impacts

- **1.2** Identify reasons for the depletion or extinction of a plant or animal species (*e.g., hunting, disease, invasive species, changes in or destruction of its habitat*), evaluate the impacts on the rest of the natural community, and propose possible actions for preventing such depletions or extinctions from happening

- **2.1** Follow established safety procedures for working with soils and natural materials (*e.g., wear gloves when handling soils to set up a working terrarium*)

- **2.2** Build food chains consisting of different plants and animals, including humans

- **2.3** Use scientific inquiry/research skills to investigate ways in which plants and animals in a community depend on features of their habitat to meet important needs (*e.g., beavers use water for shelter [they build their lodges so the entrance is under water], food [cattails, water lilies, and other aquatic plants], and protection [they slap their tails on the water to warn of danger]*)

- **2.4** Use scientific inquiry/research skills to create a living habitat containing a community, and describe and record changes in the community over time

- **2.5** Use appropriate science and technology vocabulary, including *habitat, population, community, adaptation*, and *food chain*, in oral and written communication

- **2.6** Use a variety of forms (*e.g., oral, written, graphic, multimedia*) to communicate with different audiences and for a variety of purposes (*e.g., use presentation software to show the steps one might follow to set up and maintain a terrarium*)

- **3.1** Demonstrate an understanding of habitats as areas that provide plants and animals with the necessities of life (*e.g., food, water, air, space, and light*)

- **3.2** Demonstrate an understanding of food chains as systems in which energy from the sun is transferred to producers (plants) and then to consumers (animals)

- **3.3** Identify factors (*e.g., availability of water or food, amount of light, type of weather*) that affect the ability of plants and animals to survive in a specific habitat

- **3.4** Demonstrate an understanding of a community as a group of interacting species sharing a common habitat (*e.g., the life in a meadow or in a patch of forest*)

▶

- **3.5** Classify organisms, including humans, according to their role in a food chain (*e.g., producer, consumer, decomposer*)

- **3.6** Identify animals that are carnivores, herbivores, or omnivores

- **3.7** Describe structural adaptations that allow plants and animals to survive in specific habitats (*e.g., the thick stem of a cactus stores water for the plant; a duck's webbed feet allow it to move quickly and efficiently in water*)

- **3.8** Explain why changes in the environment have a greater impact on specialized species than on generalized species (*e.g., diminishing ice cover hampers the ability of polar bears to hunt seals, their main food source, and so the polar bear population in some areas is becoming less healthy and may begin to decrease; black bear habitat has been heavily disrupted by human encroachment, but because black bears are highly adaptable omnivores that eat everything from insects to garbage generated by humans, their numbers have been increasing*)

- **3.9** Demonstrate an understanding of why all habitats have limits to the number of plants and animals they can support

- **3.10** Describe ways in which humans are dependent on natural habitats and communities (*e.g., for water, medicine, flood control in wetlands, leisure activities*)

UNIT 2: PULLEYS AND GEARS

Overall Expectations

- **1.0** Evaluate the impact of pulleys and gears on society and the environment

- **2.0** Investigate ways in which pulleys and gears modify the speed and direction of, and the force exerted on, moving objects

- **3.0** Demonstrate an understanding of the basic principles and functions of pulley systems and gear systems

Specific Expectations

- **1.1** Assess the impact of pulley systems and gear systems on daily life

- **1.2** Assess the environmental impact of using machines with pulleys and gears, taking different perspectives into account (*e.g., the perspective of a car driver or cyclist, someone who is physically challenged, the owner of a multi-floor building*), and suggest ways to minimize negative impacts and maximize positive impacts

- **2.1** Follow established safety procedures for working with machinery (*e.g., check to ensure that pulley systems are firmly attached to a secure support before operating them; be aware that changing a larger gear wheel to a smaller one will change the speed at which the mechanism moves*)

- **2.2** Use scientific inquiry/experimentation skills to investigate changes in force, distance, speed, and direction in pulley and gear systems

- **2.3** Use technological problem-solving skills to design, build, and test a pulley or gear system that performs a specific task

- **2.4** Use appropriate science and technology vocabulary, including *pulley, gear, force*, and *speed*, in oral and written communication

- **2.5** Use a variety of forms (*e.g., oral, written, graphic, multimedia*) to communicate with different audiences and for a variety of purposes (*e.g., write a set of instructions for setting up a pulley system*)

▶

- **3.1** Describe the purposes of pulley systems and gear systems (*e.g., to facilitate changes in direction, speed, or force*)

- **3.2** Describe how rotary motion in one system or its components (*e.g., a system of pulleys of different sizes*) is transferred to another system or component (*e.g., a system of various gears*) in the same structure

- **3.3** Describe how one type of motion can be transformed into another type of motion using pulleys or gears (*e.g., rotary to linear in a rack and pinion system, rotary to oscillating in a clock pendulum*)

- **3.4** Describe, using their observations, how gears operate in one plane (*e.g., spur gears, idler gears*) and in two planes (*e.g., crown, bevel, or worm gears*)

- **3.5** Distinguish between pulley systems and gear systems that increase force and those that increase speed

- **3.6** Identify pulley systems (*e.g., clotheslines, flagpoles, cranes, elevators, farm machinery*) and gear systems (*e.g., bicycles, hand drills, can openers*) that are used in daily life, and explain the purpose and basic operation of each

- **3.7** Explain how the gear system on a bicycle works (*e.g., by using the largest gear on the front chain ring and the smallest gear on the rear wheel, we can move quickly along a flat surface*)

- **3.8** Identify the input components that drive a mechanism and the output components that are driven by it (*e.g., the pedals on a bike are the input component; the rear wheel is the output component*)

UNIT 3: LIGHT AND SOUND

Overall Expectations

- **1.0** Assess the impact on society and the environment of technological innovations related to light and sound

- **2.0** Investigate the characteristics and properties of light and sound

- **3.0** Demonstrate an understanding of light and sound as forms of energy that have specific characteristics and properties

Specific Expectations

- **1.1** Assess the impacts on personal safety of devices that apply the properties of light and/or sound (*e.g., UV-coated lenses in sunglasses, safety eyes on garage door openers, reflective material on clothing, ear plugs, backup signals on trucks and cars, MP3 players, cell phones*), and propose ways of using these devices to make our daily activities safer

- **1.2** Assess the impacts on society and the environment of light and/or sound energy produced by different technologies, taking different perspectives into account (*e.g., the perspectives of someone who has to walk on the street late at night, a cottage owner, a person who is hearing impaired, manufacturers of and merchants who sell MP3 players*)

- **2.1** Follow established safety procedures for protecting eyes and ears (*e.g., use proper eye and ear protection when working with tools*)

- **2.2** Investigate the basic properties of light (*e.g., conduct experiments to show that light travels in a straight path, that light reflects off of shiny surfaces, that light refracts [bends] when passing from one medium to another, that white light is made up of many colours,* *that light diffracts [bends and spreads out] when passing through an opening)*

■ **2.3** Investigate the basic properties of sound (*e.g., conduct experiments to show that sound travels, that sound can be absorbed or reflected, that sound can be modified [pitch, volume], that there is a relationship between vibrations and sound*)

■ **2.4** Use technological problem-solving skills to design, build, and test a device that makes use of the properties of light (*e.g., a periscope, a kaleidoscope*) or sound (*e.g., a musical instrument, a sound amplification device*)

■ **2.5** Use scientific inquiry/research skills to investigate applications of the properties of light or sound (*e.g., careers where knowledge of the properties of light and/or sound play an important role [photography, audio engineering]; ways in which light and/ or sound are used at home, at school, and in the community; ways in which animals use sound*)

■ **2.6** Use appropriate science and technology vocabulary, including *natural, artificial, beam of light, pitch, loudness*, and *vibration*, in oral and written communication

■ **2.7** Use a variety of forms (*e.g., oral, written, graphic, multimedia*) to communicate with different audiences and for a variety of purposes (*e.g., create a song or short drama presentation for younger students that will alert them to the dangers of exposure to intense light and sound*)

■ **3.1** Identify a variety of natural light sources (*e.g., the sun, a firefly*) and artificial light sources (*e.g., a candle, fireworks, a light bulb*)

■ **3.2** Distinguish between objects that emit their own light (*e.g., stars, candles, light bulbs*) and those that reflect light from other sources (*e.g., the moon, safety reflectors, minerals*)

■ **3.3** Describe properties of light, including the following: light travels in a straight path; light can be absorbed, reflected, and refracted

■ **3.4** Describe properties of sound, including the following: sound travels; sound can be absorbed or reflected and can be modified (*e.g., pitch, loudness*)

■ **3.5** Explain how vibrations cause sound

■ **3.6** Describe how different objects and materials interact with light and sound energy (*e.g., prisms separate light into colours; voices echo off mountains; some light penetrates through wax paper; sound travels further in water than air*)

■ **3.7** Distinguish between sources of light that give off both light and heat (*e.g., the sun, a candle, an incandescent light bulb*) and those that give off light but little or no heat (*e.g., an LED, a firefly, a compact fluorescent bulb, a glow stick*)

■ **3.8** Identify devices that make use of the properties of light and sound (*e.g., a telescope a microscope, and a motion detector make use of the properties of light; a microphone, a hearing aid, and a telephone handset make use of the properties of sound*)

UNIT 4: ROCKS AND MINERALS

Overall Expectations

■ **1.0** Assess the social and environmental impacts of human uses of rocks and minerals

▶

■ **2.0** Investigate, test, and compare the physical properties of rocks and minerals

■ **3.0** Demonstrate an understanding of the physical properties of rocks and minerals

Specific Expectations

■ **1.1** Assess the social and environmental costs and benefits of using objects in the built environment that are made from rocks and minerals

■ 1.2 Analyze the impact on society and the environment of extracting and refining rocks and minerals for human use, taking different perspectives into account (*e.g., the perspectives of mine owners, the families of the miners, Aboriginal communities, the refinery workers, manufacturers of items who need the refined rocks and minerals to make their products, residents who live in communities located near refineries, and manufacturing facilities and who are concerned about the environment*)

■ **2.1** Follow established safety procedures for outdoor activities and for working with tools, materials, and equipment (*e.g., use scratch and streak test materials for the purposes for which they are intended; when working outdoors, leave the site as it was found*)

■ **2.2** Use a variety of tests to identify the physical properties of minerals (*e.g., hardness [scratch test], colour [streak test], magnetism*)

■ **2.3** Use a variety of criteria (*e.g., colour, texture, lustre*) to classify common rocks and minerals according to their characteristics

■ **2.4** Use scientific inquiry/research skills to investigate how rocks and minerals are used and disposed of in everyday life (*e.g., nickel and copper are made into coins; old coins can be melted down and the metal can*

be used for making other things; calcium [from limestone], silicon [from sand or clay], aluminium [from bauxite and iron ore], and iron [from bauxite and iron ore] are made into cement that is used for roads and buildings; cement can be returned to cement and concrete production facilities and recycled; rocks from quarries are used for garden landscaping, and these rocks can be reused; marble is used for countertops and statues; old and worn pieces of marble can be re-polished and re-cut to be made to look like new)

■ **2.5** Use appropriate science and technology vocabulary, including *hardness, colour, lustre*, and *texture*, in oral and written communication

■ **2.6** Use a variety of forms (*e.g., oral, written, graphic, multimedia*) to communicate with different audiences and for a variety of purposes (*e.g., use a graphic organizer to show how rocks and minerals are used in daily life*)

■ **3.1** Describe the difference between rocks (composed of two or more minerals) and minerals (composed of the same substance throughout), and explain how these differences make them suitable for human use

■ **3.2** Describe the properties (*e.g., colour, lustre, streak, transparency, hardness*) that are used to identify minerals

■ **3.3** Describe how igneous, sedimentary, and metamorphic rocks are formed (*e.g., igneous rocks form when hot, liquid rock from deep below the earth's surface rises towards the surface, cools, and solidifies; sedimentary rocks form when small pieces of the earth that have been worn away by wind and water accumulate at the bottom of rivers, lakes, and oceans and are eventually compressed*

*into rock; metamorphic rocks form when
igneous or sedimentary rocks are changed
by heat and pressure*)

- **3.4** Describe the characteristics of the
three classes of rocks (*e.g., sedimentary
rocks often have flat or curved layers, are
composed of pieces that are roughly the
same size with pores between the pieces,
and often contain fossils; igneous rocks have
no layers, are usually made up of two or
more minerals whose crystals are different
sizes, and normally do not contain fossils;
metamorphic rocks may have alternating
bands of light and dark minerals, may be
composed of only one mineral, such as
marble or quartzite, and rarely contain
fossils*), and explain how their characteristics
are related to their origin

Source: *The Ontario Curriculum, Grades 1-8: Science and Technology (2007)*

▶

Introduction

Program Principles

1. Effective science programs involve hands-on inquiry, problem solving, and decision making.

2. The development of students' skills, attitudes, knowledge, and understanding of Science, Technology, Society, and the Environment (STSE) issues form the foundation of the science program.

3. Children have a natural curiosity about science and the world around them. This curiosity must be maintained, fostered, and enhanced through active learning.

4. Science activities must be meaningful, worthwhile, and relate to real-life experiences.

5. The teacher's role in science education is to facilitate activities and encourage critical thinking and reflection. Children learn best by doing, rather than by just listening. The teacher, therefore, should focus on formulating and asking questions rather than simply telling.

6. Science should be taught in correlation with other school subjects. Themes and topics of study should integrate ideas and skills from several core areas whenever possible.

7. The science program should encompass, and draw on, a wide range of educational resources, including literature, nonfiction research material, audio-visual resources, technology, as well as people and places in the local community.

8. Assessment of student learning in science should be designed to focus on performance and understanding, and should be conducted through meaningful assessment techniques carried on throughout the unit of study.

Program Implementation

Program Resources

Hands-On Science and Technology is arranged in a format that makes it easy for teachers to plan and implement.

Units are the selected topics of study for the grade level. The units relate directly to the learning expectations outlined in *The Ontario Curriculum, Grades 1–8: Science and Technology,* 2007 document. The units are organized into several lessons. Each unit also includes books for children, a list of annotated websites, and references for teachers (all of these are found at the end of the book and are organized by unit).

The introduction to each unit summarizes the general goals for the unit. The introduction provides background information for teachers, and a complete list of materials that will be required for the unit. This includes classroom and household materials, equipment, visuals, reading materials, and various other supplies.

Each unit is organized into lessons, based on the expectations. The lessons are arranged in the following format:

Expectations: Included are the curricular expectations addressed in the lesson. Some expectations, such as those related to safety, are general, ongoing themes throughout the unit, and are not identified specifically at the beginning of a lesson.

Science Background Information for Teachers: Some topics provide teachers with the basic scientific knowledge they will need to present the activities. This information is offered in a clear, concise format, and focuses specifically on the topic of study.

Materials: A complete list of materials required to conduct the main activity is given. The quantity of materials required will depend on how you conduct activities. If students are working individually, you will need enough materials for each student. If students are working in groups, the materials required will be significantly reduced. Many of the identified items are for the teacher to use for display purposes, or for making charts for recording students' ideas. In some cases, visual materials—large pictures, sample charts, and diagrams—have been included with the activity to assist the teacher in presenting ideas and questions, and to encourage discussion. You may wish to reproduce these visuals, mount them on sturdy paper, and laminate them so they can be used for years to come.

Activity: This section details a step-by-step procedure, including higher-level questioning techniques, and suggestions, for encouraging exploration and investigation.

Activity Sheet: The reproducible activity sheets are designed to correlate with the expectations of the activity. Often, the activity sheets are to be used during the activity to record results of investigations. At other times, the activity sheets are to be used as a follow-up to the activities. Students may work independently on the sheets, in small groups, or you may choose to read through the sheets together and complete them in a large-group setting. Activity sheets can also be made into overheads or large experience charts. Since it is important for students to learn to construct their own charts and recording formats, you may want to use the activity sheets as examples of ways to record and communicate ideas about an activity. Students can then create their own activity sheets rather than use the ones provided.

Note: Activity sheets are meant to be used only in conjunction with, or as a follow-up to, the hands-on activities. The activity sheets are not intended to be the science lesson itself or the sole assessment for the lesson.

Activity Centre: Included are independent student activities that focus on the expectations.

Extensions: Included are optional activities to extend, enrich, and reinforce the expectations.

Assessment Suggestions: Often, suggestions are made for assessing student learning. These assessment strategies focus specifically on the expectations of a particular activity topic (assessment is dealt with in detail on pages 15–16). Keep in mind that the suggestions made within the activities are merely ideas to consider—you may use your own assessment techniques, or refer to the other assessment strategies on pages 15–16.

Classroom Environment

The classroom setting is an important aspect of any learning process. An active environment, one that gently hums with the purposeful conversations and activities of students, indicates that meaningful learning is taking place. When studying a specific topic, you should display related objects and materials, student work, pictures and posters, graphs and charts made during activities, and anchor charts of important concepts taught and learned. An active environment reinforces concepts and skills that have been stressed during science activities.

Timelines

No two groups of students will cover topics and material at the same rate. Planning the duration of units is the responsibility of the teacher. In some cases, the activities will not be completed during one block of time and will have to be

▶

carried over. In other cases, students may be especially interested in one topic and may want to expand upon it. The individual needs of the class should be considered; there are no strict timelines involved in **Hands-On Science and Technology**. It is important, however, to spend time on every unit in the program so that students focus on all of the curriculum expectations established for their grade level.

Classroom Management

Although hands-on activities are emphasized throughout this program, the manner in which these experiences are handled is up to you. In some cases, you may have all students manipulating materials individually; in others, you may choose to use small-group settings. Small groups encourage the development of social skills, enable all students to be active in the learning process, and mean less cost in terms of materials and equipment.

Occasionally, especially when safety concerns are an issue, you may decide to demonstrate an activity, while still encouraging as much student interaction as possible. Again, classroom management is up to you, since it is the teacher who ultimately determines how the students in his or her care function best in the learning environment.

Science Skills: Guidelines for Teachers

While involved in the activities of **Hands-On Science and Technology**, students will use a variety of skills as they answer questions, solve problems, and make decisions. These skills are not unique to science, but they are integral to students' acquisition of scientific literacy. The skills include initiating and planning, performing and recording, analyzing and interpreting, as well as communicating and the ability to work in teams. In the early years, basic skills should

focus on science inquiry. Although the wide variety of skills are not all presented here, the following guidelines provide a framework to use to encourage students' skill development in specific areas.

Observing

Students learn to perceive characteristics and changes through the use of all five senses. Students are encouraged to use sight, smell, touch, hearing, and taste (when safe) to gain information about objects and events. Observations may be qualitative (by properties such as texture or colour), or quantitative (such as size or number), or both. Observing includes

- gaining information through the senses
- identifying similarities and differences, and making comparisons
- sequencing events or objects

Exploring

Students need ample opportunities to manipulate materials and equipment in order to discover and learn new ideas and concepts. During exploration, students need to be encouraged to use all of their senses and observation skills. Oral discussion is also an integral component of exploration; it allows students to communicate their discoveries.

Classifying

This skill is used to group or sort objects and events. Classification is based on observable properties. For example, objects can be classified into living and nonliving groups, or into groups according to colour, shape, or size. One of the strategies used for sorting involves the use of Venn diagrams (either a double Venn or a triple Venn). Venn diagrams can involve distinct groups, or can intersect to show similar characteristics (please see next page).

Venn Diagram With Distinctive Groups:

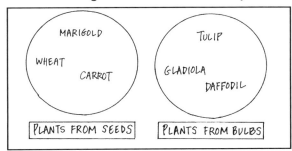

Intersecting Venn Diagram:

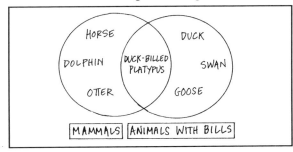

Measuring

This is a process of discovering the dimensions or quantity of objects or events and usually involves the use of standards of length, area, mass, volume, capacity, temperature, time, and speed. Measuring skills also include the ability to choose appropriate measuring devices, and using proper terms for direction and position.

In the early years, measuring activities first involve the use of *nonstandard* units of measure, such as interlocking cubes or paper clips to determine length. This is a critical preface to measuring with standard units. Once standard units are introduced, the metric system is the foundation of measuring activities. Teachers should be familiar with, and regularly use, these basic measurement units.

An essential skill of measurement is *estimating*. Regularly, students should be encouraged to estimate before they measure, whether it be in nonstandard or standard units. Estimation allows students opportunities to take risks, use background knowledge, and learn from the process.

Length: Length is measured in metres, portions of a metre, or multiples of a metre. The most commonly used units are:

- millimetre (mm): about the thickness of a paper match
- centimetre (cm): about the width of your index fingernail
- metre (m): about the length of a man's stride
- kilometre (km): 1 000 metres

Mass: Mass, or weight, is measured in grams, portions of a gram, or multiples of a gram. The most commonly used units are:

- gram (g): about the weight of a paper clip
- kilogram (kg): a cordless telephone weighs about 2 kilograms
- tonne (t): about the weight of a compact car

Note: When measuring to determine the heaviness of an object, the term *mass* is more scientifically accurate than the term *weight*. However, it is still acceptable to use the terms interchangeably in order for students to begin understanding the vocabulary of science.

Capacity: Capacity refers to the amount of fluid a container holds, and is measured in litres, portions of a litre, and multiples of a litre. The most commonly used units are:

- millilitre (mL): a soup spoon holds about 15 millilitres
- litre (L): milk comes in litre containers, or portions and multiples of a litre

Volume: Volume refers to the amount of space taken up by an object and is measured in cubic units, generally cubic centimetres (cm³) and cubic metres (m³).

▶

Note: Volume and capacity are often used interchangeably. However, a teacher should use the terms correctly in context, referring to liquid measure as capacity and space taken up as volume. Early years students are not yet expected to master the differences in the concepts and terminology, and can, therefore, be allowed to use the terms *volume* and *capacity* interchangeably.

Area: Area is measured in square centimetres, or portions and multiples thereof. By becoming familiar with the units of length, the teacher can understand area measurements by thinking of that unit in a two-dimensional form, such as square centimetres (cm^2) and square metres (m^2).

Temperature: Temperature is measured in degrees Celsius (°C). 21°C is normal room temperature; water freezes at 0°C and boils at 100°C.

Communicating

In science, one communicates by means of diagrams, graphs, charts, maps, models, symbols, as well as with written and spoken languages. Communicating includes

- reading and interpreting data from tables and charts
- making tables and charts
- reading and interpreting data from graphs
- making graphs
- making labelled diagrams
- making models
- using oral and written language

When presenting students with charts and graphs, or when students make their own as part of a specific activity, there are guidelines that should be followed:

- A *pictograph* has a title and information on one axis that denotes the items being compared. There is generally no graduated scale or heading for the axis representing numerical values.

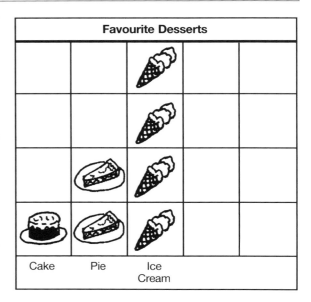

Favourite Desserts

- A *bar graph* is another common form of scientific communication. Bar graphs should always be titled so that the information communicated is easily understood. These titles should be capitalized in the same manner as one would title a story. Both axes of the graph should also be titled and capitalized in the same way. In most cases, graduated markings are noted on one axis

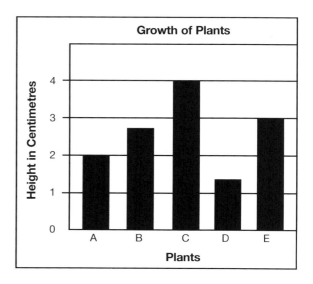

Growth of Plants

and the objects or events being compared are noted on the other. On a bar graph, the bars must be separate, as each bar represents a distinct piece of data.

■ *Charts* also require appropriate titles, and both columns and rows need specific labels. Again, all of these titles and labels require capitalization as in titles of a story. In some cases, pictures can be used to make the chart easier for young students to understand. Charts can be made in the form of checklists or can include room for additional written information and data.

Measuring Length		
Object	Estimate (cm)	Length (cm)
book	30 cm	27 cm
pencil	10 cm	16 cm

Objects in Water		
Object	Float	Sink
✂		✓
⚽	✓	

Flowers We Saw		
Type	Colour	Diagram
daffodil	yellow	🌼
rose	red	🌹
lilac	purple	🌸

Communicating also involves using the language and terminology of science. Students should be encouraged to use the appropriate vocabulary related to their investigations, for example, *objects, material, solid, liquid, gas, condensation, evaporation, magnetic, sound waves*, and *vibration*. The language of science also includes terms like *predict, infer, estimate, measure, experiment*, and *hypothesize*. Teachers should use this vocabulary regularly throughout all activities, and encourage their students to do the same. As students become proficient at reading and writing, they can also be encouraged to use the vocabulary and terminology in written form. Consider developing whole-class or individual glossaries whereby students can record the terms learned and define them in their own words.

A science and technology word wall for displaying new vocabulary is a valuable reference for students. Dedicate a classroom bulletin board to your science and technology word wall. Use index cards to record science and technology vocabulary introduced in each lesson, and attach these to the board. Encourage students to refer to the word wall during classroom activities and assignments. Also, have students record any new vocabulary in their science journals/notebooks.

▶

Predicting

A prediction refers to the question: What do you think will happen? For example, when a balloon is blown up, ask students to predict what they think will happen when the balloon is placed in a basin of water. It is important to provide opportunities for students to make predictions and for them to feel safe doing so.

Inferring

When students are asked to make an inference, it generally means that they are being asked to explain why something occurs. For example, after placing an inflated balloon in a basin of water, ask students to infer why the balloon floats. Again, it is important to encourage students to take risks when making such inferences. Before explaining scientific phenomena to students, they should be given opportunities to infer for themselves.

Investigating and Experimenting

When investigations and experiments are done in the classroom, planning and recording the process and the results are essential. There are standard guidelines for writing up experiments that can be used even with young students. Include each of these compnents in a write-up:

- purpose: what we want to find out
- hypothesis: what we think will happen
- materials: what we used
- method: what we did
- results: what we observed
- conclusion: what we found out
- application: how we can use what we learned

Researching

Even at a young age, students can begin to research topics studied in class if they are provided with support and guidelines. Research involves finding, organizing, and presenting information. For best results, teachers should always teach research skills explicitly and provide a structure for the research, indicating questions to be answered, as well as a format for conducting the research. Suggestions for research guidelines are presented regularly throughout *Hands-On Science and Technology.*

Using the Design Process

Throughout *Hands-On Science and Technology*, students are given opportunities to use the design process to design and construct objects. There are specific steps in the design process:

1. Identify a need.
2. Create a plan.
3. Develop a product.
4. Communicate the results.

The design process also involves research and experimentation.

▶

Assessment Plan

The *Hands-On Science and Technology* Assessment Plan

Hands-On Science and Technology provides a variety of assessment tools that enable teachers to build a comprehensive and authentic daily assessment plan for students.

Embedded Assessment

Assess students as they work, by using the questions provided with each activity. These questions promote higher-level thinking skills, active inquiry, problem solving, and decision making. Anecdotal Records and observations are examples of embedded assessment:

- **Anecdotal Records:** Recording observations during science activities is critical in having an authentic view of a young student's progress. The **Anecdotal Record** sheet presented on page 19 provides the teacher with a format for recording individual or group observations.

- **Individual Student Observations:** During those activities when a teacher wishes to focus more on individual students, Individual Student Observations sheets may be used (page 20). This black line master provides more space for comments and is especially useful during conferencing, interviews, or individual student presentations.

Science Journals

Have the students reflect on their science investigations through the use of **Science Journals**. Several specific samples for journalling are included with activities throughout *Hands-On Science and Technology*. Teachers can also use notebooks or the black line master provided on page 21 to encourage students to explain what they did in science, what they learned, what they would like to learn, and how they would illustrate their ideas.

Performance Assessment

Performance assessment is a planned, systematic observation and is based on students actually doing a specific science activity.

- **Rubrics:** To assess students' performance on a specific task, Rubrics are used in *Hands-On Science and Technology* to standardize and streamline scoring. A sample Rubric and a black line master for teacher use are included on pages 22 and 23. For any specific activity, the teacher selects four criteria that relate directly to the expectations of students for the specific activity being assessed. Students are then given a mark from 1–4 for each criterion accomplished, to determine a rubric score for the assessment from a total of 20 marks. These rubric scores can then be transferred to the **Rubric Class Record** on page 24.

Cooperative Skills

In order to assess students' ability to work effectively in a group, teachers must observe the interaction within these groups. A **Cooperative Skills Teacher Assessment** sheet is included on page 25 for teachers to use while conducting such observations.

Student Self-Assessment

It is important to encourage students to reflect on their own learning in science. For this purpose, teachers will find included a **Student Self-Assessment** sheet on page 26, as well as a **Cooperative Skills Self-Assessment** sheet on page 27. Of course, students will also reflect on their own learning during class discussions and especially through writing in their science journals.

▶

Science Portfolios

Select, with student input, work to include in a **Science Portfolio**. This can include activity sheets, research projects, photographs of projects, as well as other written material. Use the portfolio to reflect the student's growth in scientific literacy over the school year. Black line masters are included to organize the portfolio (**Science Portfolio Table of Contents** on page 28 and the **Science Portfolio Entry Record** on page 29).

Summative Achievement Levels

At the end of each unit, teachers can determine achievement levels for each student. All assessment tools can be used to identify these levels, referring to the chart on pages 17–18. A blackline master is included on page 30 for recording this information.

Note: In each unit of *Hands-On Science and Technology*, suggestions for assessment are provided for several lessons. Keep in mind that these are merely suggestions. Teachers are encouraged to use both the assessment strategies presented herein as well as their own valuable experience as educators in order to develop an authentic assessment plan.

▶

Achievement Chart

Categories	Level 1	Level 2	Level 3	Level 4
Knowledge and Understanding – Subject-specific content acquired in each grade (knowledge), and the comprehension of its meaning and significance (understanding)				
	The student:			
Knowledge of content (e.g., facts; terminology; definitions; safe use of tools, equipment, and materials)	demonstrates limited knowledge of content	demonstrates some knowledge of content	demonstrates considerable knowledge of content	demonstrates thorough knowledge of content
Understanding of content (e.g., concepts, ideas, theories, principles, procedures, processes)	demonstrates limited understanding of content	demonstrates some understanding of content	demonstrates considerable understanding of content	demonstrates thorough understanding of content
Thinking and Investigation – The use of critical and creative thinking skills and inquiry and problem-solving skills and/or processes				
	The student:			
Use of initiating and planning skills and strategies (e.g., formulating questions, identifying the problem, developing hypotheses, scheduling, selecting strategies and resources, developing plans)	uses initiating and planning skills and strategies with limited effectiveness	uses initiating and planning skills and strategies with some effectiveness	uses initiating and planning skills and strategies with considerable effectiveness	uses initiating and planning skills and strategies with a high degree of effectiveness
Use of processing skills and strategies (e.g., performing and recording, gathering evidence and data, observing, manipulating materials and using equipment safely, solving equations, proving)	uses processing skills and strategies with limited effectiveness	uses processing skills and strategies with some effectiveness	uses processing skills and strategies with considerable effectiveness	uses processing skills and strategies with a high degree of effectiveness
Use of critical/creative thinking processes, skills, and strategies (e.g., analysing, interpreting, problem solving, evaluating, forming and justifying conclusions on the basis of evidence)	uses critical/creative thinking processes, skills, and strategies with limited effectiveness	uses critical/creative thinking processes, skills, and strategies with some effectiveness	uses critical/creative thinking processes, skills, and strategies with considerable effectiveness	uses critical/creative thinking processes, skills, and strategies with a high degree of effectiveness
Communication – The conveying of meaning through various forms				
	The student:			
Expression and organization of ideas and information (e.g., clear expression, logical organization) in oral, visual, and/or written forms (e.g., diagrams, models)	expresses and organizes ideas and information with limited effectiveness	expresses and organizes ideas and information with some effectiveness	expresses and organizes ideas and information with considerable effectiveness	expresses and organizes ideas and information with a high degree of effectiveness

Categories	Level 1	Level 2	Level 3	Level 4
Communication (continued)				
	The student:			
Communication for different audiences *(e.g., peers, adults)* **and purposes** *(e.g., to inform, to persuade)* **in oral, visual, and/or written forms**	communicates for different audiences and purposes with limited effectiveness	communicates for different audiences and purposes with some effectiveness	communicates for different audiences and purposes with considerable effectiveness	communicates for different audiences and purposes with a high degree of effectiveness
Use of conventions, vocabulary, and terminology of the discipline in oral, visual, and/or written forms *(e.g., symbols, formulae, scientific notation, SI units)*	uses conventions, vocabulary, and terminology of the discipline with limited effectiveness	uses conventions, vocabulary, and terminology of the discipline with some effectiveness	uses conventions, vocabulary, and terminology of the discipline with considerable effectiveness	uses conventions, vocabulary, and terminology of the discipline with a high degree of effectiveness
Application – The use of knowledge and skills to make connections within and between various contexts				
	The student:			
Application of knowledge and skills *(e.g., concepts and processes, safe use of equipment and technology, investigation skills)* **in familiar contexts**	applies knowledge and skills in familiar contexts with limited effectiveness	applies knowledge and skills in familiar contexts with some effectiveness	applies knowledge and skills in familiar contexts with considerable effectiveness	applies knowledge and skills in familiar contexts with a high degree of effectiveness
Transfer of knowledge and skills *(e.g., concepts and processes, safe use of equipment and technology, investigation skills)* **to unfamiliar contexts**	transfers knowledge and skills to unfamiliar contexts with limited effectiveness	transfers knowledge and skills to unfamiliar contexts with some effectiveness	transfers knowledge and skills to unfamiliar contexts with considerable effectiveness	transfers knowledge and skills to unfamiliar contexts with a high degree of effectiveness
Making connections between science, technology, society, and the environment *(e.g., assessing the impact of science and technology on people, other living things, and the environment)*	makes connections between science, technology, society, and the environment with limited effectiveness	makes connections between science, technology, society, and the environment with some effectiveness	makes connections between science, technology, society, and the environment with considerable effectiveness	makes connections between science, technology, society, and the environment with a high degree of effectiveness
Proposing courses of practical action to deal with problems relating to science, technology, society, and the environment	proposes courses of practical action of limited effectiveness	proposes courses of practical action of some effectiveness	proposes courses of practical action of considerable effectiveness	proposes highly effective courses of practical action

Source: *The Ontario Curriculum, Grades 1-8: Science and Technology* (2007)

Date: _____   Name: _____

Anecdotal Record

Purpose of Observation: _____

Student/Group	Student/Group
Comments	**Comments**
Student/Group	**Student/Group**
Comments	**Comments**
Student/Group	**Student/Group**
Comments	**Comments**

Portage & Main Press, 2008, Hands-on Science & Technology, Grade 4, BLM, ISBN: 978-1-55379-179-9

Date: _____   Name: _____

Individual Student Observations

Purpose of Observation: _____

Student: _____
Observations
Student: _____
Observations
Student: _____
Observations

Portage & Main Press, 2008, Hands-on Science & Technology, Grade 4, BLM, ISBN: 978-1-55379-179-9

Science Journal

Date: _____ Name: _____

Today in science I _____ _____
(describe activity)

I learned _____ _____

I would like to learn more about _____ _____

Portage & Main Press, 2008, Hands-on Science & Technology, Grade 4, BLM, ISBN: 978-1-55379-179-9

- - - - ✂ -

Science Journal

Date: _____ Name: _____

Today in science I _____ _____
(describe activity)

I learned _____ _____

I would like to learn more about _____ _____

Portage & Main Press, 2008, Hands-on Science & Technology, Grade 4, BLM, ISBN: 978-1-55379-179-9

Sample Rubric

Science Activity: Looking at Minerals

Science Unit: Rocks and Minerals

Date:

4 – Full Accomplishment
3 – Substantial Accomplishment
2 – Partial Accomplishment
1 – Little Accomplishment

Student	Criteria				Rubric Score /4
	Follows Directions	Makes Detailed Observations	Sorts and Classifies Mineral Samples	Uses Appropriate Vocabulary to describe Minerals (hardness, colour, lustre, texture)	
Jarod	✓	✓	✓	—	3
Ana	✓	✓	✓	✓	4

SAMPLE

Rubric

Science Activity: _____

Science Unit: _____

Date: _____

4 – Full Accomplishment
3 – Substantial Accomplishment
2 – Partial Accomplishment
1 – Little Accomplishment

Student	Criteria				Rubric Score /4

Portage & Main Press, 2008, Hands-on Science & Technology, Grade 4, BLM, ISBN: 978-1-55379-179-9

Rubric Class Record

Student	Unit/Activity/Date									
	Rubric Scores /4									

Scores on Specific Tasks	Achievement Level
1	Level 1
2	Level 2
3	Level 3
4	Level 4

Portage & Main Press, 2008, Hands-on Science & Technology, Grade 4, BLM, ISBN: 978-1-55379-179-9

Cooperative Skills
Teacher Assessment

Date: _____

Task: _____

_____

Group Member	Cooperative Skills				
	Contributes ideas and questions	Respects and accepts contributions of others	Negotiates roles and responsibilities of each group member	Remains focused and encourages others to stay on task	Completes individual commitment to the group

Comments: _____

_____

_____

Portage & Main Press, 2008, Hands-on Science & Technology, Grade 4, BLM, ISBN: 978-1-55379-179-9

Date: _____   Name: _____

Student Self-Assessment

Looking at My Science Learning

1. What I did in science: _____

_____

_____

2. In science I learned: _____

_____

_____

3. I did very well at: _____

_____

_____

4. I would like to learn more about: _____

_____

_____

5. One thing I like about science is: _____

_____

_____

Portage & Main Press, 2008, Hands-on Science & Technology, Grade 4, BLM, ISBN: 978-1-55379-179-9

Date: _____   Name: _____

Cooperative Skills Self-Assessment

Students in my group:

_____   _____

_____   _____

Group Work – How Did I Do Today?

Group Work	How I Did (✔)		
	🙂	😐	🙁
I shared ideas.			
I listened to others.			
I asked questions.			
I encouraged others.			
I helped with the work.			
I stayed on task.			

I did very well in _____

_____

Next time I would like to do better in _____

_____

Portage & Main Press, 2008, Hands-on Science & Technology, Grade 4, BLM, ISBN: 978-1-55379-179-9

Date: _____   Name: _____

Science Portfolio Table of Contents

Entry	Date	Selection
1.	_____	_____
2.	_____	_____
3.	_____	_____
4.	_____	_____
5.	_____	_____
6.	_____	_____
7.	_____	_____
8.	_____	_____
9.	_____	_____
10.	_____	_____
11.	_____	_____
12.	_____	_____
13.	_____	_____
14.	_____	_____
15.	_____	_____
16.	_____	_____
17.	_____	_____
18.	_____	_____
19.	_____	_____
20.	_____	_____

Portage & Main Press, 2008, Hands-on Science & Technology, Grade 4, BLM, ISBN: 978-1-55379-179-9

Date: _____   Name: _____

Science Portfolio Entry Record

This work was chosen by _____

This work is _____

_____

I chose this work because _____

_____

_____

_____

_____

- ✂ - - -

Date: _____   Name: _____

Science Portfolio Entry Record

This work was chosen by _____

This work is _____

_____

I chose this work because _____

_____

_____

_____

Portage & Main Press, 2008, Hands-on Science & Technology, Grade 4, BLM, ISBN: 978-1-55379-179-9

Summative Achievement Levels

Student	Achievement Levels			
	Unit 1: _____	Unit 2: _____	Unit 3: _____	Unit 4: _____

Portage & Main Press, 2008, Hands-on Science & Technology, Grade 4, BLM, ISBN: 978-1-55379-179-9

Understanding Life Systems

Unit 1: Habitats and Communities

Books for Children

Caduto, Michael, J. *Keepers of the Animals: Native American Stories and Wildlife Activities for Children*. Golden, CO: Fulcrum, 1997.

Cherry, Lynne. *The Great Kapok Tree: A Tale of the Amazon Rain Forest*. San Diego: Harcourt Brace Jovanovich, 1990.

Chinery, Michael. *Wild Animal Planet: Animal Habitats*. London, UK: Southwater, 2008.

Eyvindson, Peter. *Jen and the Great One*. Winnipeg, MB: Pemmican Publications, 1990.

Godkin, Celia. *Wolf Island*. Markham, ON: Fitzhenry & Whiteside, 1993.

Kelley, Dr. Alden. *A Tree Is a Home*. Learn to Read Science Series Level 3. Cypress, CA: Creative Teaching Press, 1997.

McLellan, Joe. *Nanabosho: How the Turtle Got Its Shell*. The Nanabosho Series. Winnipeg, MB: Pemmican Publications, 1990.

Ryder, Joanne. *Chipmunk Song*. New York: E.P. Dutton, 1987.

Schwartz, David. *Among the Flowers*. Look Once, Look Again Science Series. Cypress, CA: Creative Teaching Press, 1997.

_____. *At the Farm*. Look Once, Look Again Science Series. Cypress, CA: Creative Teaching Press, 1997.

_____. *At the Pond*. Look Once, Look Again Science Series. Cypress, CA: Creative Teaching Press, 1997.

_____. *At the Zoo*. Look Once, Look Again Science Series. Cypress, CA: Creative Teaching Press, 1997.

_____. *In a Tree*. Look Once, Look Again Science Series. Cypress, CA: Creative Teaching Press, 1997.

Schwartz, David. *In the Desert*. Look Once, Look Again Science Series. Cypress, CA: Creative Teaching Press, 1997.

_____. *In the Forest*. Look Once, Look Again Science Series. Cypress, CA: Creative Teaching Press, 1997.

_____. *In the Garden*. Look Once, Look Again Science Series. Cypress, CA: Creative Teaching Press, 1997.

_____. *In the Meadow*. Look Once, Look Again Science Series. Cypress, CA: Creative Teaching Press, 1997.

_____. *In the Park*. Look Once, Look Again Science Series. Cypress, CA: Creative Teaching Press, 1997.

_____. *The Seashore*. Look Once, Look Again Science Series. Cypress, CA: Creative Teaching Press, 1997.

_____. *Underfoot*. Look Once, Look Again Science Series. Cypress, CA: Creative Teaching Press, 1997.

Slade, Suzanne. *What Do You Know About World Habitats?* New York: PowerKids Press, 2008.

Stetson, Emily. *Kid's Easy-to-Create Wildlife Habitats*. Nashville, TN: Williamson Books, 2004.

Stubbendieck, James, et al. *North American Wildland Plants: A Field Guide*. Lincoln, NE: University of Nebraska Press, 2003.

Van Allsburg, Chris. *Just a Dream*. Boston: Houghton Mifflin, 1990.

Websites

■ <http://www.seedsfoundation.ca/greenschools.html>

Society, Environment, and Energy Development site: Become an Environmental Green School, and join the 4 500 schools across Canada that are currently registered in this program (also called Learners Action).

■ <http://www.lifelab.org/>

The Life Lab Science Program researches and develops curriculum for elementary school science by using a Living Laboratory school garden. Selected as a "Center of Excellence" by the National Science Teachers Association (NSTA) and the National Science Foundation (NSF).

■ <http://www.wwfcanada.org/>

World Wildlife Fund Canada is an outstanding educational resource for students and teachers. Through "Teachers and Kids," and "Schools for a Living Planet," order free teaching materials supporting WWF's Schools for Wildlife program.

■ <http://www.spca.bc.ca/Kids/default.asp>

Education Division of the British Columbia Society for the Prevention of Cruelty to Animals: An exceptional website for teachers: includes pet care guidelines for all kinds of pets and guidelines for pets in the classroom.

■ <http://www.bearden.org/>

The Bear Den: For teachers and students who are researching bears, this website includes information on population and distribution, vital statistics, physical characteristics, diet and food sources, reproduction, mortality, and hibernation— for eight species of bears.

■ <http://www.fi.edu/tfi/units/life/life.html>

Franklin Institute Science Museum: An excellent site for researching living things with extensive cross-links and links to various resources. Find sites for classification, adaptation, ecosystems, biomes, habitats, the life cycle, survival, the food chain, and the energy cycle.

■ <http://www.seaworld.org/>

Sea World website: The animal Info link is specifically designed to help you quickly find information about the animal kingdom. Site includes scientific classifications (click on "Animal Bytes"), ecology and conservation, and "fun zone."

■ <http://www.gov.mb.ca/conservation/wildlife/managing/snakes.html>

Visit the Narcisse Snake Dens. Click on "Frequently asked questions" for information on the snakes, predators, and more.

■ <http://www.web.net/~greentea/>

Green Teacher Magazine is written by and for teachers committed to environmental and global education. Includes online articles such as "Re-mystifying the City," "Waste Reduction," "The Outdoor Classroom," and much more. *Green Teacher* also offers extensive links.

■ <http://kids.nationalgeographic.com/Animals/CreatureFeature/Polar-bear>

Part of the National Geographic Kids site, this page about polar bears includes information on population and distribution, vital statistics, physical characteristics, diet and food sources, reproduction, mortality, and hibernation. The page includes video clips, games, and more.

Introduction

In this unit, students will become familiar with the basic needs of plants and animals. They will explore and compare ways in which communities of plants and animals meet their needs in specific habitats.

Throughout this unit, students will investigate the concepts of *habitat* and *community*, and identify the factors that could affect habitats and communities of plants and animals. They will also investigate the dependency of plants and animals on their habitat and the interrelationships of the plants and animals living in a specific habitat. Students will also describe ways in which humans can change habitats and the effects of these changes on the plants and animals within the habitats.

There is no better way to motivate students to learn about animals than to have a live animal in the classroom. Students will find all concepts and objectives in this unit more meaningful if they have an animal to observe and care for.

Many animals are suitable for the classroom, and are relatively easy to look after. Fish, for example, are easily cared for, and a fish tank provides an excellent observation centre for students. Guinea pigs are also appropriate animals for the classroom; they are large enough for students to handle, are not fast enough to escape, and are often gentle and affectionate. To introduce a greater variety of animals to the classroom, you may also choose to have guest pets, such as a bird, a rabbit, a gerbil, a snake, and so on, visit the classroom for short periods of time.

Note: Students' allergies should be considered before you select a classroom animal, but should not prevent you from introducing another appropriate animal to the class.

To provide students with hands-on experiences, you will need to have living plants in the classroom. Collect a variety of plants that students can care for. Also, plant seeds so that students can observe population growth. Plant slips may also be brought from home to start new plants.

To teach this unit, you will need many pictures, books, and films depicting plant and animal populations, habitats, and relationships within environmental communities. Involve students in this project. Good sources for photographs and drawings are:

- old calendars
- magazines, especially *Ranger Rick, Owl, Chickadee, Highlights for Children,* and *National Geographic*
- departments of agriculture
- gardening magazines
- seed catalogues
- forestry and environmental associations
- Greenpeace
- local zoological, wildlife, humane, and naturalist societies

If you contact groups, such as those named above, in advance, many will provide booklets, posters, and information. Some may also provide kits or presentations for classrooms.

Put together a collection of several fiction and nonfiction books about animals. Keep these in a separate part of your classroom library or at the plant and animal centres where they can be referred to during activity, research, and free times.

Science Vocabulary

Throughout this unit, teachers should use, and encourage students to use, vocabulary such as: *habitat, population, community, adaptation, food chain, producer, consumer, herbivore, carnivore, omnivore, food web, scavenger, endangered species, extinct species,* and *technology.*

A science and technology word wall for displaying new vocabulary is a valuable reference for students. Dedicate a classroom bulletin board to your science and technology word wall. Use index cards to record science and technology vocabulary introduced in each lesson, and attach these to the board. Encourage students to refer to the word wall during classroom activities and assignments. Also, have students record any new vocabulary in their science journals/notebooks.

Materials Required for the Unit

Classroom: chart paper, felt markers, pencils, large sheets of art paper, markers, coloured pencils, oil pastels, scissors, glue, index cards, art paper, mural paper, construction paper, masking tape, clipboards, field guides (sample included), paint, crayons

Books, Pictures, and Illustrations: books about and magazines with pictures of different animals and plants and their habitats (e.g., forest, river, pond, marsh, desert, prairie, city, mountains, ocean), various books on plants and animals in different habitats, large food cycle chart (depicting producers, consumers, and decomposers; sample included), two pictures illustrating food chains (included), *Chipmunk Song* (a book by Joanne Ryder), books on uses of animals and plants and other research resources, *Wolf Island* (a book by Celia Godkin), (books and pictures about bear species (polar bear, grizzly bear, black bear), newspapers and magazines, field guides for plants, books about eating habits of animals, informational books about habitats and their populations

Household: string, paper bag, plastic bag, circle tracers (such as margarine tub lids or paper plates)

Other: various waste materials such as lettuce leaves, apples cores, bread, containers for creating habitats, plant materials for habitat, animal(s) for habitat, nature walk recording sheet (sample included), coloured wool or string

A Note About Materials

The materials needed to complete some activities are extensive. Teachers should review the materials lists for the unit ahead of time and make a note of items that students may be able to bring from home (for example, plastic containers, paper plates and/or cups, spoons, pie plates, fabric samples, balls of wool). Then, prior to beginning the lesson, teachers can send a letter home with students asking parents/guardians to donate some of these materials.

A Note About Safety

During their exploration of habitats and communities, students should be able to identify, and understand, the practices that ensure their own safety and the safety of others. This includes knowing why it is important that they wash their hands before and after handling plants and animals, and properly clean and maintain the environment for all plants and animals brought into the classroom.

1 Habitats

Expectations

- **2.5** Use appropriate science and technology vocabulary, including *habitat, population, community, adaptation*, and *food chain*, in oral and written communication

- **2.6** Use a variety of forms to communicate with different audiences and for a variety of purposes

- **3.1** Demonstrate an understanding of habitats as areas that provide plants and animals with the necessities of life

- **3.4** Demonstrate an understanding of a community as a group of interacting species sharing a common habitat

Materials

- chart paper
- markers
- books or magazines with pictures of different habitats (e.g., forest, river, pond, marsh, desert, prairie, city, mountains, ocean)

Activity

Have a class discussion on the needs of plants and animals. Encourage students to provide their ideas of what all animals and plants need in order to survive. Focus on the importance of factors such as food, water, shelter, and space. Have students discuss the various places where plants and animals live, such as in a forest, a pond, a marsh, a prairie, or a city. Ask:

- What is the name for the place where an animal or plant lives?

Focus on the concept of *habitat*, encouraging students to explain what a habitat is. Provide examples of animals and plants and their natural habitats. Explain that when plants and animals live together in a certain area, they make up a *population*. Ask:

- What does the habitat provide for animal and plant populations?
- Can a population get its food from within the habitat?
- Can a population get its water, shelter, and space from within the habitat?

Divide the class into four equal groups. Have each group go to a different corner of the classroom. Clear a space in the centre of the room. Explain to students that each group is going to represent one important factor to an animal's survival in its habitat (for example, group one: food; group two: water; group three: shelter; group four: space).

Have one student from each group walk toward the centre of the room. Tell the four students to stand next to each other (in order by group number), facing inward. Have four more students (one from each group) join the first four students by standing at the right shoulder of the first member of their group. In this manner, keep adding groups of four students until all students have formed one big circle.

Ask students to turn to the right and take one step toward the centre of the circle. They should be standing close together, still in a circle. Each student should be looking at the back of the head of the person in front of him/her. The toes of each student should be almost touching the heels of the student in front.

Make sure students are listening carefully. Have them put their hands on the shoulders of the person in front of them. Then, tell students that, on the count of three, they are to sit down on the lap of the person behind them. Remind students to keep their knees together to support the person in front of them. Once students are sitting in the lap circle say:

- Food, water, shelter, and space are needed to have a suitable habitat.

1

At this point, have students stand up, fall, or sit down to get out of the lap circle. Once students' laughter has subsided, ask:

- What are the necessary components of a habitat?
- What would happen to the lap circle if one of the components was missing?
- What would happen to a habitat if one of the components was missing?

Have students try the lap circle again. This time, have the water students identify themselves. Say:

- It is a drought year. The water supply has been diminished by a drought.

Have the water students leave the circle. After the circle collapses, ask:

- Why did the circle collapse?
- Can you think of anything else that would impact a habitat? (for example, pollution of water supply, soil erosion, urban development, destruction of woodland communities)

Select one of the habitat pictures to study as a class. Have students identify the habitat, describe it, and list the plant and animal populations that would live in this habitat.

Divide the class into small groups. Give each group a picture of a habitat. Ask the students to:

- identify the habitat and describe it
- name the animal populations that would live in the habitat
- name the plant populations that would live in the habitat

Distribute Activity Sheet A (1.1.1), and have students record their findings on their activity sheets. Distribute new copies of the activity sheet, and rotate the pictures. Have each group examine several different habitats.

Activity Sheet A

Note: Have students complete the activity sheet during the lesson rather than as a follow-up to the lesson. Make several copies for each student.

Directions to students:

Print the name of the habitat on the activity sheet, describe the habitat, and list plant and animal populations that would live in this habitat. Repeat for a different habitat picture on a new activity sheet (1.1.1).

Extensions

- Take a trip to a zoo to examine how the zoo tries to make animals' habitats much like their natural habitats.

- If you have a classroom animal, discuss how students have attempted to make the animal's home much like its natural habitat.

- Have groups of students make large murals depicting different habitats. Then, have each group make a list of things that will support the growth of all living things in the habitat they have selected.

- Have each student draw a picture of his/her local habitat (community). Ask students to list the important components of their habitat for humans, as well as the source of each of these components (e.g., shelter: house; food: grocery store, farms, markets).

Assessment Suggestion

Provide students with several pictures of animals, and have them identify habitats where the animals could survive. Also, have students identify the important components of a habitat that help the animal to survive there. Use the Anecdotal Record sheet, found on page 19, to record results.

Date: _____

Habitats

Habitat: _____

Description	Plant and Animal Populations

2 | Why Plants and Animals Live in Certain Habitats

Expectations

- **2.5** Use appropriate science and technology vocabulary, including *habitat, population, community, adaptation*, and *food chain*, in oral and written communication

- **2.6** Use a variety of forms to communicate with different audiences and for a variety of purposes

- **3.1** Demonstrate an understanding of habitats as areas that provide plants and animals with the necessities of life (e.g., food, water, air, space, and light)

- **3.3** Identify factors that affect the ability of plants and animals to survive in a specific habitat

Materials

- large collection of pictures of animals and plants living in different habitats (e.g., city, desert, ocean, field, forest, mountains, pond)
- chart paper
- markers
- variety of informational books about habitats and their populations

Activity

Ask students:

- Do you remember what the needs are of all living things?
- What are these needs? (air, water, food, and shelter)
- Can you recall the components of an animal habitat? (food, water, shelter, and space)

Record the needs of living things and the components of an animal habitat on chart paper.

Display the pictures of animals and plants for students to observe. Ask students:

- Where does each animal live?

- Where does each plant live?
- How are these habitats different from each other?

On chart paper, print the name of each animal and plant pictured and the habitat in which it lives.

Classify the plants and animals according to their habitats.

Now, have students focus on each animal/plant individually. Ask:

- Why would this animal/plant live in this habitat?
- What needs of this animal/plant can be met by living in this habitat?
- What do you think would happen if this animal/plant was taken out of its habitat?
- In what other habitats could this animal/plant live?
- Which habitats would not be good for the animal/plant?

Activity Sheet A

Note: Encourage students to refer to informational books to determine the characteristics of certain habitats and the needs of populations within these habitats.

Directions to students:

Record the name of a plant or animal, along with its habitat. Draw a diagram showing the plant/animal in its habitat. Explain why the plant/animal lives in the habitat that it does (that is, why the habitat suits the plant/animal) (1.2.1).

Extensions

- Collect calendar pictures of various habitats. Have some students sort the pictures while others guess their sorting rule (for example, forest, ocean, desert).

2

- Together with students, brainstorm lists of describing words for various habitat pictures, and have students use the words to write poems. Then, have students make line drawings or watercolour paintings to illustrate their poems.

- Challenge students to design and construct models (dioramas) of local or regional habitats and their associated populations of plants and animals. Have students use shoeboxes and natural materials to create their models (dioramas). Then, have them use play dough or modelling clay to make plants and animals that live in the habitat.

Date: _____

Name: _____

Why Do They Live Where They Live?

Population: _____

Habitat: _____

Diagram:

How the Habitat Suits the Plant/Animal

Portage & Main Press, 2008, Hands-on Science & Technology, Grade 4, BLM, ISBN: 978-1-55379-179-9

2A

3 Investigating Local Habitats

Expectations

- **2.5** Use appropriate science and technology vocabulary, including *habitat, population, community, adaptation*, and *food chain*, in oral and written communication

- **2.6** Use a variety of forms to communicate with different audiences and for a variety of purposes

- **3.4** Demonstrate an understanding of a community as a group of interacting species sharing a common habitat

Materials

- clipboards
- pencils
- field guides for plants (*e.g., North American Wildland Plants: A Field Guide*, a book by James Stubbendieck et al)
- collection of books on plants and animals
- sample nature walk recording sheets (included) (1.3.1)

Note: Clipboards can be made with a piece of cardboard and a clothespin. You may wish to use a string to attach the pencil to the clipboard.

Activity: Part One

Note: Before going on a nature hike, review with students the importance of respecting the environment and of leaving it the way they found it.

Tell students that they are going to go on a nature walk of a local habitat near the school. Explain that the purposes of the trip are to (a) observe many different types of plants and animals in a local habitat, and (b) classify the plants and animals they see based on similarities and differences.

Before going on the walk, ask students to decide how they will record what they see.

Ask:

- How can you record your observations in an organized manner?
- How can you sort or classify the things you see?

Brainstorm a list of ways to categorize observations. For example:

- plants and animals
- trees, plants, and grasses
- mammals, insects, and spiders (and so on)
- large plants and small plants
- green plants and non-green plants
- aquatic plants and land plants

Next, design the recording sheet together on chart paper (a two-page sample is included, 1.3.1). Then, make a smaller version of the recording sheet, and photocopy one for each student, or have students draw their own from the class model on chart paper.

Activity: Part Two

Give each student (or pair of students) a clipboard and a pencil.

Review the recording sheet with students, then take them to a local habitat. Review boundaries for observation. Also, remind students of safety rules. Ask:

- What are some plants that are dangerous to humans? (poison ivy, poison sumac, sharp needles of some weeds and plants)
- Why are these plants dangerous?
- What happens if a human comes in contact with these plants?
- What safety rules should you remember to follow when you go on your nature walk?
- Why are some animals dangerous to humans? (animals could have rabies, fleas, diseases, or students could be allergic to specific animals)

3

- What happens if humans come in contact with these animals?
- What safety rules should you remember to follow when you go on your nature walk?

Have students observe plants and animals in the designated habitat and record their findings on their recording sheets.

Note: Students should be encouraged to observe carefully and draw the specimens they see, especially those that they cannot identify. Explain that botanists, for example, keep detailed diagrams and drawings of unusual flora. They can then compare their drawings and notes about a specimen with a field guide in order to identify it.

Back in the classroom, have students share their findings. Use the master recording sheet on chart paper to record their findings.

Discuss with students that when plants and animals form a community, they share a common habitat. Have students brainstorm other habitats they might find locally (for example, life in a meadow, life in a forest).

Challenge students to find the names of plants and animals they observed on their nature walk. Provide a collection of books on plants and animals for students to locate information. When students have found the name of a particular plant or animal, have them complete Activity Sheet A (1.3.2). Later, collect these pages, and bind them into a book called *Plants and Animals in Our Local Habitat*.

Activity Sheet A

Directions to students:

Choose a plant or animal you observed on your nature walk. Research the plant or animal, and record your research on the field guide record form (1.3.2).

Activity: Part Three

Explain to students that they are going to go back to the local habitat they visited earlier and conduct a second investigation. This time, they will be trying to determine the most appropriate method for measuring a plant population in its local habitat.

Have students select one plant population to investigate (for example, grass, ferns, dandelions, elm trees). Brainstorm a list of ways to measure the population of this plant in its local habitat. For example:

- Conduct an exact population count by sectioning the area and having groups do a count within each section.

- Conduct a sample population count by doing a population count within a small section of the site (such as 10 square metres). Use the sample population count to calculate a total population count by measuring the total area and then determining the fraction of this total area used for the sample. Then, multiply the sample counted by the denominator to calculate the total population count.

Record the suggestions. As a class, discuss the pros and cons of each method. Agree on a method to use for conducting a population count of a specific plant.

Divide the class into small groups. Give each group a clipboard and a copy of Activity Sheet B (1.3.3). Return to the local habitat. Using the method agreed on in class, have each group estimate and count the population of the plant.

Back in the classroom, record the results of each group on chart paper. Compare the results. Ask students:

- Were your results similar to the results of the other groups?

■ Why do you think they were similar? Why do you think they were different?

■ How can you use these results to decide on a class result? (average the findings)

Activity Sheet B

Directions to students:

On the activity sheet, record the population you measured, your estimate of the population, the method you used to measure it, and the results. Also, draw a diagram of the plant (1.3.3).

Extensions

■ Invite a local botanist, naturalist, gardener, landscaper, wildlife expert, or the owner of a plant shop into the classroom to speak to students about local plants and animals.

■ Have students conduct research projects on the risks to humans posed by certain plants or animals (for example, Lyme disease, poison ivy, hay fever, rabies).

■ Graph the findings from Activity Sheet B (1.3.3) for each group, as well as the class average.

■ Divide the class into groups. Have each group measure the population of a different plant in the same local habitat. Compare the size of different populations in your local habitat. Graph your findings.

Assessment Suggestion

Observe students during the nature walk. Focus on their ability to observe the natural environment, record their findings, identify their observations, and discuss their ideas. Use the Rubric sheet, found on page 23, to list these (or other) criteria and record results.

Sample Nature Walk
Recording Sheet

Describe your nature walk habitat. _____

_____

_____

_____

Trees	Small Plants

Mammals	Insects	Spiders

Portage & Main Press, 2008, Hands-on Science & Technology, Grade 4, BLM, ISBN: 978-1-55379-179-9

Date: _____   **Name:** _____

Interesting Things I Observed on Our Nature Walk

Portage & Main Press, 2008, Hands-on Science & Technology, Grade 4, BLM, ISBN: 978-1-55379-179-9

Date: _____   **Name:** _____

Field Guide Record Form

Name of plant/animal: _____

Description of plant/animal: _____

_____

_____

Diagram of plant/animal:

Habitat: _____

_____

_____

Other Observations: _____

_____

_____

_____

_____

3A

Portage & Main Press, 2008, Hands-on Science & Technology, Grade 4, BLM, ISBN: 978-1-55379-179-9

Date: _____ Name: _____

Population of _____
in Our Local Habitat

Population estimate: _____

Method used to measure the population:

Diagram

_____

_____

_____

_____

_____

_____

_____

_____

_____

Results: _____

_____

_____

_____

_____

_____

_____

Portage & Main Press, 2008, Hands-on Science & Technology, Grade 4, BLM, ISBN: 978-1-55379-179-9

4 Plant and Animal Adaptations

Expectations

- **2.5** Use appropriate science and technology vocabulary, including *habitat, population, community, adaptation*, and *food chain*, in oral and written communication

- **2.6** Use a variety of forms to communicate with different audiences and for a variety of purposes

- **3.7** Describe structural adaptations that allow plants and animals to survive in specific habitats

- **3.8** Explain why changes in the environment have a greater impact on specialized species than on generalized species

Science Background Information for Teachers

Adaptations allow plants and animals to survive in their habitats. Structural adaptations include physical features that protect a living thing, help it get its food, or help it to move. For example, a hawk has a hooked beak that can rip and tear food, and a sparrow has a short, pointed beak that can crack open seeds. Water birds have flat beaks that allow them to scoop food from the water.

Body colour is another form of adaptation that protects animals by camouflaging them.

The different characteristics of three bear species provide examples of ways animals have adapted to their environments.

Polar Bears

- have long slender necks, slender heads (for searching for seals in holes in ice)
- black skin (absorbs heat from the sun)
- live in the Arctic (mostly on polar ice)
- feed on fish and seals

- have thick fur (to provide warmth)
- have webbing between toes (for swimming)

Grizzly Bears

- have long claws (dig up most of their food)
- have distinctive hump between shoulders (hump is a muscle mass for powering forelimbs)
- eat roots, gophers, smaller rodents (occasionally kill larger animals for food)
- live on edges of forest
- feed mostly in mountain meadow

Black Bears

- are quiet, shy animals
- live in a variety of habitats (forests, brush, or chaparral)
- eat nuts, berries, fruit, rodents, insects (occasionally larger animals)
- smaller than polar and grizzly bears (also have more pointed heads)

Materials

- books on polar bears, grizzly bears, and black bears
- pictures of bear species (polar bear, grizzly bear, black bear)
- chart paper
- markers
- books and pictures of a variety of plants and animals in different habitats

Activity

Note: This activity may take place over several class periods as you study the adaptations of living things.

Show the pictures of the bears to students. Ask:

- How are these bears alike?
- How are these bears different?

Read informational books about polar bears, grizzly bears, and black bears.

Write the name of each bear on a separate sheet of chart paper. Record the physical characteristics of each bear, as well as information about each bear's habitat.

Encourage students to look at similarities and differences in the physical appearances of the bears, as well as those of their habitats. Ask:

■ Think about how each bear looks. Does the bear's physical characteristics help it to survive where it lives?

■ Think about what each bear eats. Why does it eat this food? What physical characteristics help it get the food it eats?

■ What are the needs of the grizzly bear? How does a grizzly bear meet its needs in its habitat?

■ What are the needs of a polar bear? How does a polar bear meet its needs in its habitat?

■ What are the needs of a black bear? How does a black bear meet its needs in its habitat?

■ If someone took polar bears to a national park in central Canada and took grizzly bears to the Arctic coast, do you think the bears would be able to survive in their new homes? Why or why not?

List students' responses on the appropriate sheet of chart paper.

Explain to students that these bears have adapted to their environments in order to survive. All plants and animals need to make some adaptations in order to survive.

Explain that changes in the environment have a greater impact on specialized species of animals than on generalized species.

Divide the class into small groups, and provide each group with chart paper, markers, and books and pictures of plants and animals. Have the groups review several books and observe pictures to identify ways that animals and plants have adapted to their habitats. Examples may include:

■ The snowshoe rabbit has a white coat in winter and a tan coat in summer to help it blend in with its surroundings.

■ Chameleons change colour to blend in with their surroundings.

■ Cacti have fleshy stems to hold water during periods of drought.

■ The height of a plant depends on the amount of sunlight it gets and needs.

■ A walking stick insect looks like a twig or stick, which helps to protect it from enemies.

Have each group present its findings to the class. Display the charts in the classroom, and encourage students to add to the lists throughout the unit.

Activity Sheet A

Directions to students:

Use the chart to record examples of how animals and plants adapt to survive in their environments (1.4.1).

Activity Sheet B

Directions to students:

Select a plant or animal, and write its name at the top of the page. Draw a diagram of your plant or animal in its habitat. Label the plant or animal's physical characteristics that help it to adapt to its habitat (1.4.2).

4

Extensions

■ Investigate alternate explanations of plant and animal adaptations, based on traditional knowledge from a variety of cultures. For example, read Aboriginal legends that explain how animals and plants got their unique features. After reading stories from several cultures and examining the features of this type of text, have students write their own legends. Examples may include
  ■ How the skunk got its stripe
  ■ How the giraffe got its long neck
  ■ How the fox got its bushy tail
  ■ Why the polar bear is white
  ■ How the cactus got its needles
  ■ How the porcupine got its quills
  ■ Why the sunflower turns to the sun

Note: An excellent resource for this project is *Keepers of the Animals*, a book by Michael J. Caduto.

■ Investigate ways that technological developments mirror physical adaptations. For example, scuba fins are much like a duck's webbed feet, a fishing net is similar to a spider's web, and an airplane is designed much like the body of a bird. Have students identify human designs that reflect things in nature. Have them fold a piece of art paper in half, and draw the human design on one half (such as an airplane) and the natural phenomenon on the other half (such as a bird). These pages can be put together into a class book titled *Mirror Images*.

Date: _____

Name: _____

Adaptations

Animal/Plant	Adaptation	Why the Adaptation Is Important to Its Survival

Date: _____   Name: _____

Adapting to the Environment

Name of plant or animal: _____

Portage & Main Press, 2008, Hands-on Science & Technology, Grade 4, BLM, ISBN: 978-1-55379-179-9

5 | Relationships Within a Community

Expectations

- **2.3** Use scientific inquiry/research skills to investigate ways in which plants and animals in a community depend on features of their habitat to meet important needs

- **2.5** Use appropriate science and technology vocabulary, including *habitat, population, community, adaptation,* and *food chain,* in oral and written communication

- **2.6** Use a variety of forms to communicate with different audiences and for a variety of purposes

- **3.4** Demonstrate an understanding of a community as a group of interacting species sharing a common habitat

Materials

- chart paper
- markers
- mural paper
- art supplies (e.g., paint, coloured pencils)
- pieces of wool (various colours)

Activity: Part One

Review what a habitat is. Have students brainstorm a list of different habitats. Record each habitat on a separate sheet of chart paper. Under each habitat, list the animals and plants that would be found there.

Review that when living things of the same type live together in an area, they make up a *population* (for example, geese in a pond, beavers in a lake, wildflowers in a field). When a number of populations live together in one habitat (such as in a forest), a *community* is formed.

Focus on one habitat, such as a forest.

Ask students:

- How do you think populations within a forest community affect one another?
- Where do animals get food to eat within the forest community?
- How does this affect the plants and other animals in the community?
- What would happen if all the trees in the forest died?
- How would this affect the other populations?
- What would happen if the insects in a forest died?
- How would this affect the other populations?
- How do animals depend on other populations to build their homes? (e.g., beaver dams, birds' nests, spiders' webs, burrows, humans' houses)

Now, focus on the interdependence of populations in the forest. Stress that all the populations in a community affect one another. Focus on communities in other habitats (listed on separate sheets of chart paper) in the same manner.

Discuss communities within a human habitat, such as in a town, village, or city. Ask:

- How are humans affected if trees become diseased?
- What would happen to humans if their vegetable gardens and crops were eaten by grasshoppers?
- In what other ways are humans affected by other populations in their community? (Talk about mosquitoes, aphids, gophers, and so on.)

Activity: Part Two

Divide the class into working groups, and have each group select a community to illustrate on a mural. When the groups have completed the murals, have them use coloured wool to connect each animal to all parts of the community to which it relates. Tell students to use different colours of wool for each animal, connecting the animal to the populations it uses for food and the populations with which it shares its home.

Activity Sheet A

Note: This is a two-page activity sheet.

Directions to students:

Read each story. List the possible reasons for the population increase or decrease in each community. Explain the effects of the population increase or decrease on other plant and animal populations within the community (1.5.1).

Extensions

■ Have students research an endangered species. They can describe how it has become endangered, the effects of its endangerment on other animals in its communities, and what humans are doing to protect the animal.

■ Have students write local and national officials to ask the status of endangered species in Ontario and elsewhere in Canada.

■ Have students write or email local, national, and international environmental organizations requesting information on what can be done to protect threatened or endangered species in your area.

■ As a class, read *Wolf Island,* a book by Celia Godkin. It is an excellent story depicting the relationships within a community. *The Great Kapok*, a book by Lynne Cherry, is another excellent story relating to this concept.

Date: _____   Name: _____

Relationships Within a Community: Changes in Populations

Life in Shady Forest

Once upon a time, there was a small forest teeming with animals and plants. There were pine and oak trees, shrubs, grasses, flowers, squirrels, birds, and insects of all kinds. There was also a great number of deer—428, in fact! Ten years later, the plant and animal populations in Shady Forest had changed greatly. For example, only 126 deer were now living in the forest.

1. Record possible reasons for the decrease in the deer population.

_____

_____

_____

2. What effect might the decrease in the deer population have on other plant/animal populations in the habitat?

_____

_____

_____

Portage & Main Press, 2008, Hands-on Science & Technology, Grade 4, BLM, ISBN: 978-1-55379-179-9

Life in Lake Nosbonsing

Once upon a time, there was a lake filled with living things. Frogs, water insects, beavers, ducks, loons, and all kinds of fish, including 85 pickerel, were living in the lake. Over the years, the lake community changed. Fifteen years later, there were 359 pickerel in Lake Nosbonsing.

1. Record possible reasons for the increase in the pickerel population.

_____

_____

_____

2. What effect might the increase in the pickerel population have on other plant/animal populations in the habitat?

_____

_____

_____

5A

Portage & Main Press, 2008, Hands-on Science & Technology, Grade 4, BLM, ISBN: 978-1-55379-179-9

6 Herbivores, Carnivores, and Omnivores

Expectations

- **2.5** Use appropriate science and technology vocabulary, including *habitat, population, community, adaptation*, and *food chain*, in oral and written communication

- **2.6** Use a variety of forms to communicate with different audiences and for a variety of purposes

- **3.6** Identify animals that are carnivores, herbivores, or omnivores

Science Background Information for Teachers

An animal that eats only plants is called an *herbivore*. An animal that eats only animals/meat is called a *carnivore*. An animal that eats both plants and animals is called an *omnivore*.

Materials

- books on animals that focus, in part, on their eating habits
- pencils

Activity

Divide the class into groups, and provide students with Activity Sheet A (1.6.1), pencils, and books about animals.

Challenge students to use the books to research the eating habits of animals. Explain that some animals eat only plants. These animals are called *herbivores*. Animals that eat only meat are called *carnivores*, and animals that eat both plants and meat are called *omnivores*. Add the words herbivore, carnivore, and omnivore, along with a definition of each, to your science word wall. Ask:

- On your activity sheet, under which heading would you put humans?
- What plants do humans eat?
- What animals do humans eat?

Have students list humans under the column titled "Omnivore." Then, in their groups, have students continue to research eating habits of other animals. For visual reinforcement, students may wish to draw each animal beside its name on the chart.

Activity Sheet A

Note: This activity sheet is to be used during the lesson rather than as a follow-up to the lesson.

Directions to students:

Record the names of herbivores, carnivores, and omnivores (1.6.1).

Activity Centre

Print the names of several herbivores, carnivores, and omnivores on cards, and have students play a variation of the card game "Go Fish." Deal each player six cards. The objective is to collect three cards with the names of animals belonging to one classification (such as carnivores). When asking another player for a card, the student asks, "Do you have an omnivore (or carnivore or herbivore)?" If the other player has an omnivore card, he or she must hand it over. If not, the player selects a card from the deck. When any player has a set of three cards, the cards can be placed on the table. The game is over when one player has placed all his/her cards in sets on the table and has none in his/her hand.

Extensions

- Have students draw pictures of various herbivores, carnivores, and omnivores. Under each illustration, students can describe the classification and eating habits of the animal. For example:

  - A rabbit is a herbivore.
  - A rabbit eats grass, leaves, and vegetables.

6

Collect the sheets, classify them, and bind them into three books—one on herbivores, one on carnivores, and a third on omnivores.

- If you have a classroom pet, have students design a test to find out if the animal is a herbivore, carnivore, or omnivore.

- Visit a local zoo. Give each student a clipboard and pencil, and have students record the names of five carnivores, five omnivores, and five herbivores that they observe at the zoo.

Assessment Suggestion

Meet with students individually, and have each student sort the cards from the card game "Fish" into each of the three categories: herbivores, omnivores, and carnivores. Use the Anecdotal Record sheet, found on page 19, to record results.

Date: _____   Name: _____

Herbivores, Carnivores, and Omnivores

An animal that eats only plants is called a herbivore.

An animal that eats only meat is called a carnivore.

An animal that eats both plants and animals is called an omnivore.

Herbivore	Carnivore	Omnivore

Portage & Main Press, 2008, Hands-on Science & Technology, Grade 4, BLM, ISBN: 978-1-55379-179-9

7 | Create Your Own Living Habitat

Expectations

- **2.4** Use scientific inquiry/research skills to create a living habitat containing a community, and describe and record changes in the community over time

- **2.5** Use appropriate science and technology vocabulary, including *habitat, population, community, adaptation*, and *food chain*, in oral and written communication

- **2.6** Use a variety of forms to communicate with different audiences and for a variety of purposes

Materials

- students' completed activity sheets from lesson 6
- containers (for creating a terrarium or aquarium)
- plant materials appropriate for a habitat
- animals appropriate for a habitat
- chart paper
- marker
- books and magazines about plants and animals and their habitats

Note: In small groups, students will be using their inquiry skills to create a living habitat containing a community. Students will also describe and record changes in the community over time. Stress to students that all living creatures introduced into the habitat have to be humanely sustained, and remind them that the animals will be returned to their natural habitat at the end of the unit.

Some appropriate animals for the habitat are mealworms, butterflies, snails, and ants. As well, you may want to purchase animals such as Leopard Gecko lizards, which you can keep in a classroom-maintained habitat throughout the school year. This is a very effective way to watch the changes in the animal and the habitat for a prolonged period of time.

Activity

Review with students what a habitat is. Have students brainstorm a list of possible habitats that they would like to create. Record students' ideas on chart paper. Ask students:

- What factors do you need to consider when you are setting up your habitat? (e.g., location of container, creating the right climate, light and humidity)
- What equipment and materials will you need to create a habitat that meets the needs of the community it is going to support? (for example, container of the right size, appropriate plants and/or animals)

Distribute Activity Sheet A (1.7.1) to students. In small groups, have students plan the habitats they want to create and list the materials they will need on their activity sheets. Provide several periods of class time to allow the groups to research their habitats and come up with suitable plans.

Next, have the groups create their habitats. Give students several weeks to observe and record changes in the communities they have built. To conclude this lesson, ask

- What did you learn from your early observations about meeting the needs of living things?
- As you observed your habitat over a period of time, what modifications, or changes, did you need to make in order to keep the habitat healthy?

Activity Sheet A

Note: This is a three-page activity sheet.

Directions to students:

Use the activity sheet to create a plan for a living habitat containing a community (1.7.1).

My Living Habitat

Project Planning

Type of habitat I will create: _____

Materials I need:

_____   _____

_____   _____

_____   _____

Procedure

This is a labelled diagram/sketch of my habitat:

Portage & Main Press, 2008, Hands-on Science & Technology, Grade 4, BLM, ISBN: 978-1-55379-179-9

Collecting and Presenting Data

This is what I learned from my early observations about meeting the needs of living things:

_____

_____

_____

Based on my observations, I have made the following changes to keep the habitat healthy:

_____

_____

_____

_____

Results — Analyzing and Reporting

This is what happened to the community living in the habitat I made:

_____

_____

_____

_____

Portage & Main Press, 2008, Hands-on Science & Technology, Grade 4, BLM, ISBN: 978-1-55379-179-9

This is what I learned:

_____

_____

_____

_____

This is what I could do differently next time if I were to create another habitat.

_____

_____

_____

_____

_____

Conclusion

_____

_____

_____

_____

_____

Portage & Main Press, 2008, Hands-on Science & Technology, Grade 4, BLM, ISBN: 978-1-55379-179-9

8 | Producers, Consumers, and Decomposers

Expectations

- **2.2** Build food chains consisting of different plants and animals, including humans

- **2.5** Use appropriate science and technology vocabulary, including *habitat, population, community, adaptation*, and *food chain*, in oral and written communication

- **2.6** Use a variety of forms to communicate with different audiences and for a variety of purposes

- **3.5** Classify organisms, including humans, according to their role in a food chain

Science Background Information for Teachers

Producers are living things (such as plants) that become food for other living things. They are called producers because they are able to produce their own food. *Consumers* are animals that eat producers and/or other consumers. Animals that eat plants are called *first-order consumers*. Animals that eat first-order consumers are called *second-order consumers*. Animals that eat second-order consumers are called *third-order consumers*, and so on. *Decomposers* are tiny plants and animals that feed on the wasted products of consumers, thereby converting that waste, as well as dead animals and plants, into material that is returned to the soil.

Materials

- Activity Sheet A (1.6.1) from lesson 6 (completed by students)
- large food-cycle chart depicting producers, consumers, and decomposers (see right)
- markers
- various waste materials (e.g., lettuce leaves, apple cores, bread)
- paper bag

- plastic bag
- chart paper

Activity: Part One

Review the activity sheet from lesson 6 completed by students (1.6.1). Reproduce the food-cycle chart below on chart paper. Focus on the eating habits of each group. Ask students:

- What do herbivores eat?

Explain that plants manufacture their own food from the elements in soil, water, air, and from the sun, and also provide food for other living things. Plants are called *producers*.

Food Cycle

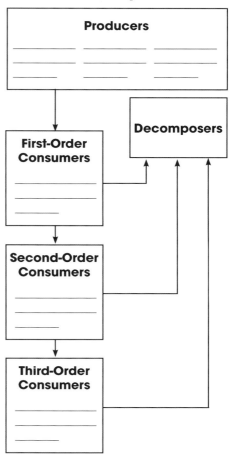

8

Have students brainstorm a list of producers. Record their ideas in the appropriate box on the food-cycle chart. Ask:

■ Do animals make their own food?
■ From where do they get their food?

Stress that since animals cannot make their own food, they must eat plants and other animals. Animals are called *consumers,* because they consume food from other living things rather than produce their own food. Animals that eat plants are called *first-order consumers*. Ask:

■ Which animals are first-order consumers? (plant eaters)

Have students brainstorm a list of first-order consumers, and record their ideas in the box titled "First-Order Consumers." Explain that animals that eat first-order consumers are called *second-order consumers*. Point to the list of first-order consumers, and ask:

■ Which animals eat these first-order consumers?

List students' responses under the heading "Second-Order Consumers." Ask:

■ What do you call animals that eat second-order consumers?
■ What animals can you name that eat these second-order consumers?

On the chart, list the names of third-order consumers under the heading, "Third-Order Consumers."

Note: Students will realize that some animals can be considered first-, second-, and third-order consumers. For example, humans eat plants, but also eat first- and second-order consumers. Therefore, humans will be listed under all three headings.

Activity: Part Two

Focus on decomposers. Ask students:

■ What do you think happens to plants and animals after they die?
■ What happens to the garbage that you throw away every day?

Have students design an experiment to find out what happens to waste materials. For example:

Place a piece of bread inside a plastic bag, and observe the growth of mould and the eventual decomposition of the bread.

or

Place lettuce leaves, apple cores, and other plant material in a paper bag, and bury it in the ground. Wait at least a week, dig up the bag, and observe the decomposition.

Focus again on the food-cycle chart. Explain that tiny plants and animals are found in the soil. These living things are called *decomposers*. They change waste products from producers and consumers into materials that go back into the soil. This process helps producers make more food so that the cycle of life can continue.

Activity Sheet A

Directions to students:

Read and complete the sentences at the top of the page. Complete the chart, showing a producer and several consumers. Also, read and answer the questions at the bottom of the page (1.8.1).

Extensions

■ Have students write a paragraph comparing producers, consumers, and decomposers. This offers an opportunity to integrate literacy skills and concepts.

8

Note: The following extension activities promote environmental awareness.

- As a class, visit a landfill site, and find out how waste material is disposed of. Then, have students predict which wastes will decompose and which wastes will not decompose.

- Encourage students to start a compost at home and use the decomposing material in gardens. If you have a flower bed or garden at school, consider making a compost. Students can participate by bringing waste material from home for the compost. In turn, gardens and flower beds can be fertilized with the decomposing material.

- Start a recycling and compost program at school. Have students sort the garbage from their snacks and lunches into three piles (recyclable, compost, garbage). Make a compost in a back corner of the schoolyard. Use the decomposing material to fertilize gardens and flower beds at school.

- As a class, visit a mushroom farm to learn how decomposers are used to grow this food.

Assessment Suggestions

- Have students divide a piece of paper into four equal parts. Label the parts in the following order: "Producer," "First-Order Consumer," "Second Order Consumer," and "Third Order Consumer." Ask students to illustrate and label examples for each heading. Use the Rubric sheet, found on page 23, to record results.

Note: The four criteria on the rubric may include:
1. examples of producers
2. examples of first-order consumers
3. examples of second-order consumers
4. examples of third-order consumers

- Conference with students on an individual basis. Show pictures of various plants and animals. Have each student identify the plant or animal in each picture as a producer, consumer, or decomposer. Use the Individual Student Observations sheet, found on page 20, to record results.

Producers, Consumers,
and Decomposers

Green plants are _____.
They make their own food.

_____ **are animals that eat producers
and other consumers. They cannot make their own food, so they
must eat other things.**

Complete the flow chart to show a producer and several consumers.

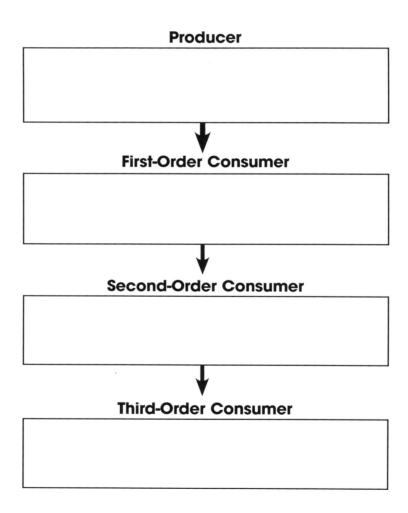

Producer

First-Order Consumer

Second-Order Consumer

Third-Order Consumer

What are decomposers? _____

How do decomposers help other populations? _____

_____

Portage & Main Press, 2008, Hands-on Science & Technology, Grade 4, BLM, ISBN: 978-1-55379-179-9

9 | Food Chains

Expectations

- **2.2** Build food chains consisting of different plants and animals, including humans

- **2.5** Use appropriate science and technology vocabulary, including *habitat, population, community, adaptation*, and *food chain*, in oral and written communication

- **2.6** Use a variety of forms to communicate with different audiences and for a variety of purposes

- **3.2** Demonstrate an understanding of food chains as systems in which energy from the sun is transferred to producers (plants) and then to consumers (animals)

Science Background Information for Teachers

A food chain is an excellent way to illustrate the direct line of energy transferred from the sun to a plant (producer), to consumers, and to decomposers.

Materials

- 2 pictures illustrating food chains (included) (They can be copied onto overhead transparencies or used as is.) (1.9.1, 1.9.2)
- chart paper
- felt markers
- large sheets of art paper
- circle tracers (e.g., margarine tub lids, paper plates)
- art supplies (e.g., glue, scissors, pencil crayons, oil pastels)

Activity: Part One

Display the first picture, illustrating a food chain (1.9.1). Ask students:

- What do you think this diagram is describing?

- Which living thing in this picture is a producer?
- Which living thing is a first order consumer?
- Is the first order consumer a herbivore, omnivore, or carnivore?
- Which living thing is a second order consumer?
- Is the second order consumer a herbivore, omnivore, or carnivore?

Explain that the diagram shows how living things interact through a food chain. Ask students:

- How does the corn get its food?
- Why is the sun important to the food chain?
- Which living things eat the corn?
- Which living thing eats the chicken?
- How does the cycle go back to the corn?
- What happens to the waste material from humans?

Focus on decomposers and on how they break down human waste material and return it to the soil, so that the waste can be used by the plants again. Ask:

- What would happen if the corn was removed from the food chain?
- What would happen if the chicken was removed from the food chain?

Repeat the activity, using the second food chain diagram (1.9.2).

Activity: Part Two

Brainstorm other food chains, and list them on chart paper.

Have each student create a food chain: trace circles on a sheet of art paper, draw appropriate living things inside each circle, and connect the circles to show the relationships. Title the illustration "Food Chain."

Have each student present his/her diagram to the class and describe the relationships illustrated.

Activity Sheet A

Directions to students:

Use the diagram provided to create a food chain. Label your food chain with producers and consumers. Read and answer the questions at the bottom of the page (1.9.3).

Extension

Provide numerous pictures of living things, and have students use the pictures to make food chains. This activity also works well at an activity centre, as it can be done independently.

Assessment Suggestions

■ Evaluate the food-chain charts presented by the students. Break the evaluation down into two components: content (accuracy of the food chain, ability to answer questions asked), and presenting skills (voice quality, eye contact). Use the Individual Student Observations sheet, found on page 20, to record results.

■ Have students complete the Student Self-Assessment sheet, found on page 26, to reflect on their own learning about food chains.

Food Chain 1

DECOMPOSERS

Portage & Main Press, 2008, Hands-on Science & Technology, Grade 4, BLM, ISBN: 978-1-55379-179-9

Food Chain 2

DECOMPOSERS

Food Chain

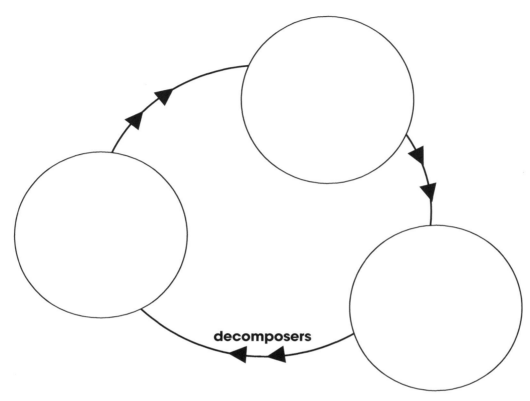

decomposers

1. What would happen if the producer in your food chain died?

_____

_____

_____

2. How would this affect the first-order consumer in the food chain?

_____

_____

_____

3. What would happen if the population of the second-order consumer increased? _____

_____

_____

Portage & Main Press, 2008, Hands-on Science & Technology, Grade 4, BLM, ISBN: 978-1-55379-179-9

10 Food Webs

Expectations

- **2.2** Build food chains consisting of different plants and animals, including humans

- **2.5** Use appropriate science and technology vocabulary, including *habitat, population, community, adaptation*, and *food chain*, in oral and written communication

- **2.6** Use a variety of forms to communicate with different audiences and for a variety of purposes

Materials

- *Chipmunk Song,* a book by Joanne Ryder
- coloured wool or string
- chart paper
- felt markers
- index cards
- food-chain charts (created by students in lesson 9)

Activity

Read aloud *Chipmunk Song* to students. Following the story, have students brainstorm a list of all of the animals pictured in the book. Record the list on chart paper. Go through the list, and ask students:

- Which animals eat only plants?
- What are these animals called?
- What different plant sources are mentioned in the book? (Record these plant sources on the chart paper.)
- Can you find an animal on the list that would eat another animal on the list?
- Are there any other examples of animals on the list that would eat other animals on the list?

Assign each student a plant or animal from the list. Have students write the name of their plant or animal on an index card. Explain that they are going to represent the plant or animal on their index card.

Now, tell students they are going to find out how a food web works. Have students stand in a semicircle. Ask each "animal" what plant or animal it would eat. Run a piece of coloured string (or wool) between the "animal" and its food source. Once all "animals" are connected to their food source, ask:

- What do you notice about the plants and animals in this semicircle?
- How are the plants and animals interdependent?
- Can you find a food chain in this semicircle?
- Can you find other food chains?
- Are these food chains related in any way?

Explain to students that when food-chains are connected to other food chains, a *food web* is created.

Have students focus on the food-chain charts they created in the previous lesson. Discuss how different food chains could be related.

Activity Sheet A

Directions to students:

Complete the food web by drawing pictures of living things that could be placed in each empty circle of the web. Complete the sentences that describe the food web (1.10.1).

Extension

Have students glue the food-chain charts they created in the previous activity onto a larger sheet of paper and draw a second food chain above or below the original food chain. Then, have them draw lines to show how the two food chains are related and label the large sheets, "Food Web."

10

Assessment Suggestion

Have students present their food webs to the class and describe the relationships shown. Evaluate content (knowledge of concept) and presentation skills (voice quality, eye contact). Use the Anecdotal Record sheet, found on page 19, to record results.

Food Webs

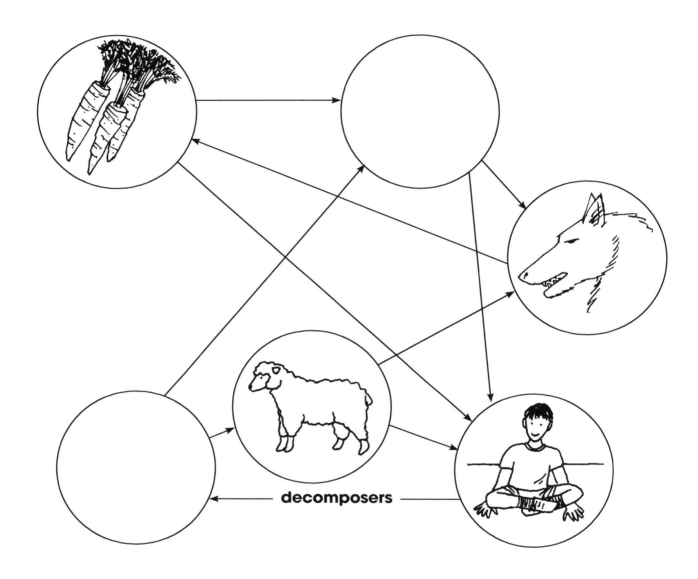

decomposers

Use the above food web to help you complete the sentences.

Carrots are eaten by_____. _____ are

eaten by wolves. _____ is eaten by sheep. Sheep

are eaten by humans. Carrots are also eaten by _____.

Sheep are also eaten by_____.

Portage & Main Press, 2008, Hands-on Science & Technology, Grade 4, BLM, ISBN: 978-1-55379-179-9

11 | Importance of Plants and Animals to Humans

Expectations

- **2.5** Use appropriate science and technology vocabulary, including *habitat, population, community, adaptation*, and *food chain*, in oral and written communication

- **2.6** Use a variety of forms to communicate with different audiences and for a variety of purposes

- **3.10** Describe ways in which humans are dependent on natural habitats and communities

Materials

- chart paper,
- markers
- art paper
- magazines, newspapers
- glue
- scissors
- books on uses of animals and plants (from local and school library), and other research resources

Activity: Part One

As a class, discuss the importance of plants and animals to humans. Ask:

- How are plants important to us?
- What do they give us? (e.g., oxygen, food, medicines, cloth, dyes, lumber)
- How are animals important to us?

Divide the class into small groups (three or four students per group). Give each group a sheet of chart paper and a marker. Have each group brainstorm a list (using words or pictures) of ways in which humans use plants, animals, plant products, and animal products.

Once each group has completed their list, post the lists at the front of the classroom, and review them together. Explain to students how dependent humans are on plants and animals.

Have students work together in their groups and use pictures from magazines and newspapers to make collages, that illustrate plant and animal products on which humans depend.

Display the collages in the classroom.

Activity: Part Two

In pairs, have students select one item from the lists (generated in Activity: Part One) to research. Students might research an animal product (such as eggs, bacon, milk, yogurt, ham, beef, or leather) or a plant product (such as fruits, vegetables, cloth, lumber, or medicines). Provide resources for students to use to gather information (for example, nonfiction books, brochures, CDs, bookmarked sites on the Internet).

Tell students they are responsible for researching the following:

- which plant/animal their item comes from
- where the plant is grown or where the animal comes from (where it is raised)
- what part of the plant/animal is used
- what the plant/animal looks like
- showing how the plant/animal is used
- the positive and negative impacts of humans on the natural habitat of the plant/animal

Once students have completed their research, have them display their findings in an interesting way and present their findings to the class.

Display the research projects in the classroom or at the school library.

▶

11

Activity Sheet A

Note: This a three-page activity sheet.

Directions to students:

Use the research guide to plan your research on your plant or animal (1.11.1).

Extension

Investigate ways that plants and animals are used in other cultures. For example, research Aboriginal uses for plants and animals. Consider inviting an Aboriginal elder to your class to discuss traditional knowledge with students. Also, focus on the cultural importance of plant and animal populations and interactions.

Assessment Suggestions

■ Assess students' oral presentations and their final research projects. As a class, you can develop a class rubric for the presentation. Be sure to develop the assessment criteria together (for example, quality of voice, information presented, visual effects). Record results on the Rubric sheet, found on page 23, then transfer to the Rubric Class Record sheet, found on page 24.

■ Have students complete a Student Self-Assessment sheet, found on page 26, to reflect on their own learning while conducting the research project.

My Research Project

Research Checklist

Research Topic: _____

My research includes:

1. **Which plant/animal the item comes from** ❑

2. **Where the plant is grown/where the animal comes from** ❑

3. **What part of the plant/animal is used** ❑

4. **An illustration of the plant/animal** ❑

5. **A picture of how the plant/animal is used** ❑

6. **The positive and negative impacts of humans on the natural habitat of my plant/animal** ❑

7. **My time-management record** ❑

8. **My rough notes (information gathering)** ❑

Portage & Main Press, 2008, Hands-on Science & Technology, Grade 4, BLM, ISBN: 978-1-55379-179-9

Keeping My Research on Track

Time-Management Record

Date	Length of Time	What I Accomplished

Portage & Main Press, 2008, Hands-on Science & Technology, Grade 4, BLM, ISBN: 978-1-55379-179-9

Date: _____ Name: _____

Information Gathering

Topic: _____

Resources Used:

11A

Portage & Main Press, 2008, Hands-on Science & Technology, Grade 4, BLM, ISBN: 978-1-55379-179-9

12 Natural and Human Effects on Plants, Animals, and the Environment

Expectations

- **1.1** Analyze the positive and negative impacts of human interactions with natural habitats and communities, taking different perspectives into account, and evaluate ways of minimizing the negative impacts

- **2.5** Use appropriate science and technology vocabulary, including *habitat, population, community, adaptation*, and *food chain*, in oral and written communication

- **2.6** Use a variety of forms to communicate with different audiences and for a variety of purposes

Materials

- chart paper
- *Just a Dream*, a book by Chris Van Allsburg
- pencils
- markers

Activity: Part One: Environmental Issues

Read aloud *Just a Dream*. As a class, discuss the environmental issues presented in the book.

Activity: Part Two: Human Effects

Before starting this activity, divide a sheet of chart paper into two columns labelled "Humans Helping the Environment" and "Humans Harming the Environment."

Divide the class into working groups, and provide each group with Activity Sheet A (1.12.1) and pencils.

Challenge the groups to brainstorm a list of ways in which humans affect the environment. Ask students:

- What are some good things human do for the environment?
- How do humans help their own population when they take care of the environment?

- What are some bad things that humans do to the environment?
- How do these things harm plants and animals?
- How do humans harm their own population when they harm the environment?

Have the group members work cooperatively to record their lists on the activity sheet chart.

As the groups present their lists to the class, record their ideas on chart paper.

Focus on the list of harmful actions by humans. Ask:

- What are some solutions to these harmful things that humans are doing to plants, animals, and the environment?
- How can you help protect plants and animals and conserve the environment?

Activity: Part Three: Natural Effects

Once you have created a list of solutions to harmful actions by humans, ask students:

- Are there other things harmful to populations, communities, and the environment that are beyond human control?

Have students brainstorm a list of natural disasters. Divide a sheet of chart paper into two columns. Title the first column "Natural Disasters." These may include droughts, floods, increase/decrease in one population that affects another population. Focus on issues that have occurred in your area, such as ice storms, heat waves, floods, and so on, and discuss how these events have affected plant and animal populations.

Label the second column "Effects on Plants and Animals," and record students' ideas in this column.

12

Activity Sheet A

Note: This activity sheet is to be used during the activity rather than as a follow-up.

Directions to students:

Read the sentences at the top of the page. On the chart, record your ideas of how humans help and harm the environment (1.12.1).

Extensions

- Have students brainstorm ways they can donate their time as service to the environment. Examples include:

  - organizing the recycling program at school
  - participating in a garbage cleanup
  - volunteering at a local wildlife conservation area or bird sanctuary
  - starting an advertising campaign in the local or school community on heightening awareness of pollution

  Students can select one way to provide service to the environment, explain how they will provide this service, and record the amount of time they volunteered to this service on the Extension activity sheet (1.12.2).

- Have students research endangered and extinct plants and animals. Have students create murals of living things that are endangered or extinct. Contact organizations that are attempting to improve the plight of these plants and animals.

- Start a recycling project at school, focusing on reusable items. Brainstorm for things that are used in the classroom such as paper, large envelopes, picture magazines, and containers of different sizes, and attempt to obtain a supply of these items.

- Organize classroom or school-wide fund-raisers, and donate all proceeds to a local environmental foundation.

- As a class, visit a wildlife conservation area or bird sanctuary to observe how humans are attempting to protect the environment.

- Investigate ways that technology is used to increase humans' understanding of plant and animal life, such as time-lapsed photography, radio collar tracking, and computer mapping of migratory birds. These technological developments are often used to study plants and animals to ensure their survival, and to reduce endangerment and extinction of species.

- Participate in community cleanup projects.

- Have students design posters that help to heighten awareness of pollution.

- Research acid rain. Observe the effects of acid rain by spraying a plant with a solution of water and vinegar (which is an acid). This will affect the plant much like acid rain does.

Date: _____   Name: _____

Human Effects on the Environment

Humans interact with the environment in many ways. Some human actions are helpful to populations in the environment. Some human actions are harmful to populations in the environment.

Record human actions that help and harm populations in the environment.

How Humans Help Populations in the Environment	How Humans Harm Populations in the Environment

Portage & Main Press, 2008, Hands-on Science & Technology, Grade 4, BLM, ISBN: 978-1-55379-179-9

Date: _____   Name: _____

Service to the Environment

My service to the environment is: _____

I will provide this service by: _____

_____

I think this service is important because: _____

_____

_____

Volunteer Record

Date	Time	What I Did

Portage & Main Press, 2008, Hands-on Science & Technology, Grade 4, BLM, ISBN: 978-1-55379-179-9

13 | Changes in the Environment

Expectations

- **1.2** Identify reasons for the depletion or extinction of a plant or animal species, evaluate the impacts on the rest of the natural community, and propose possible actions for preventing such depletions or extinctions from happening

- **2.5** Use appropriate science and technology vocabulary, including *habitat, population, community, adaptation*, and *food chain*, in oral and written communication

- **2.6** Use a variety of forms to communicate with different audiences and for a variety of purposes

- **3.8** Explain why changes in the environment have a greater impact on specialized species than on generalized species

- **3.9** Demonstrate an understanding of why all habitats have limits to the number of plants and animals they can support

Materials

- chart paper
- marker
- *Wolf Island*, a book by Celia Godkin

Activity: Part One

Explain to students that they are going to explore reasons for the depletion or extinction of an animal species. As a class, discuss how the following practices have impacted the wolf population of Ontario:

- deforestation (for land development)
- hunting and trapping (to increase tourism)

Record students' ideas on chart paper. Then, ask:

- Can one change in a food web affect an entire community?

Have students evaluate how depletion/extinction impacts the rest of the natural community. Hold a class discussion on ways humans can prevent depletions/extinctions from happening.

Activity: Part Two

Read aloud *Wolf Island*. Following the reading, have a class discussion about the changes that took place on the island after the wolves were removed. Then, distribute Activity Sheet A (1.13.1), and have students complete the food web and explain, in their own words, how the change in the wolf population affected the island population.

Activity Sheet A

Note: This is a two-page activity sheet.

Directions to students:

On page 1, draw an *X* overtop the wolves to show their depletion. Put a "+" or "–" on the line above each producer or consumer to show if its population went up or down after the wolves were removed.

On page 2, use information from the story *Wolf Island* and your own ideas to help you write a paragraph explaining how the population on Wolf Island was affected by the removal of the wolves. Be sure to include how other plants and animals would be affected by the removal of the wolves. Also, suggests ways humans could help these remaining plants and animals survive (1.13.1).

Wolf Island

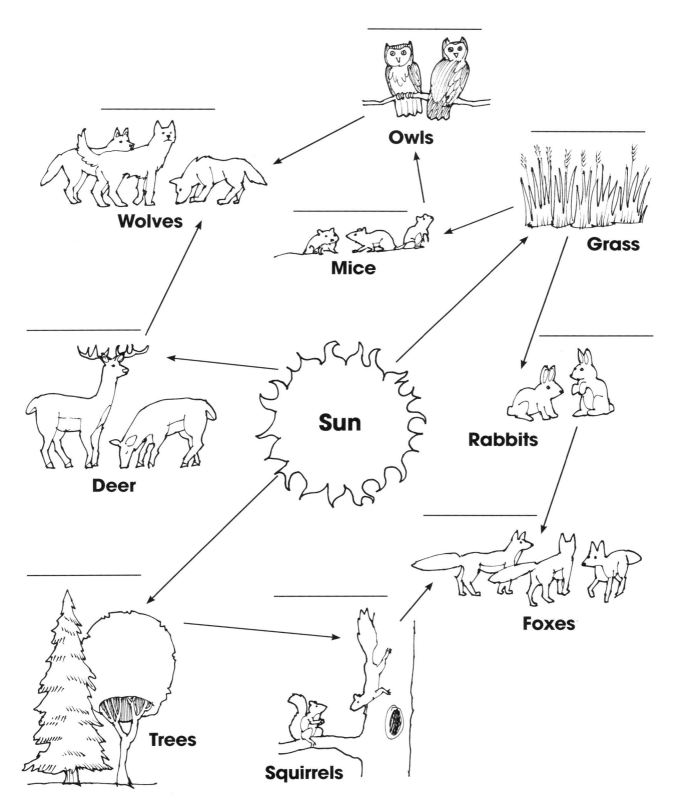

Portage & Main Press, 2008, Hands-on Science & Technology, Grade 4, BLM, ISBN: 978-1-55379-179-9

Explain how changing one part of a food web can affect many different populations. Use evidence from the story *Wolf Island* and your own ideas to support your answer.

_____

_____

_____

_____

_____

_____

_____

_____

_____

_____

_____

_____

_____

_____

_____

_____

_____

_____

References for Teachers

Burnie, David. *Forest*. New York: Dorling Kindersley, 1998.

_____. *Tree*. New York: Knopf, 1988.

Butzow, Carol, and John Butzow. *Science Through Children's Literature*. Englewood, NJ: Teacher Ideas Press, 1989.

Canadian Wildlife Federation. *Project Wild: Elementary Activity Guide*. Ottawa, 1989.

Carratello, John, and Patty Carratello. *Plants*. Huntington Beach: Teacher Created Materials, 1998.

Chandler, Pauline. *Ecology*. Huntington Beach: Teacher Created Materials, 1994.

Conway, Lorraine. *Plants*. Upper Saddle River, NJ: Good Apple, 1980.

Forman, Michael. *Arctic Tundra*. Habitats series. New York: Children's Press, 1997.

_____. *Douglas Fir*. Habitats series. New York: Children's Press, 1997.

_____. *Suguaro Cactus*. Habitats series. New York: Children's Press, 1997.

Greenaway, Theresa. *Swamp Life*. New York: Dorling Kindersley, 1993.

Hickman, Pamela. *The Kids Canadian Plant Book*. Toronto: Kids Can Press, 1996.

Orenstein, Ronald. *How on Earth? A Question-and-Answer Book About How Animals and Plants Live*. Toronto: Key Porter Books, 1994.

Parker, Steve. *Eyewitness Natural World*. New York: Dorling Kindersley, 1994.

_____. *Pond & River*. Eyewitness Books. Toronto: Knopf, 1988.

Rubenstein, Len, and Ellen Doris. *The Big Book of Nature Projects*. New York: Thames & Hudson, 1997.

Suzuki, David. *Looking at Plants*. Toronto: Stoddart, 1985.

Taylor, Barbara. *Cave Life*. Look Closer series. Toronto: Stoddart, 1992.

_____. *Forest Life*. Look Closer series. Toronto: Stoddart, 1992.

_____. *Meadow*. Look Closer series. Toronto: Stoddart, 1992.

_____. *Pond Life*. Look Closer series. Toronto: Stoddart, 1992.

_____. *River Life*. Look Closer series. Toronto: Stoddart, 1992.

_____. *Swamp Life*. Look Closer series. Toronto: Stoddart, 1992.

_____. *Tree Life*. Look Closer series. Toronto: Stoddart, 1992.

Time-Life Books. *Photographing Nature*. Alexandria, VA: Time-Life Books, 1981.

Understanding Structures and Mechanisms

Unit 2: Pulleys and Gears

Books for Children

Barton, Byron. *Machines at Work*. New York: Crowell, 1987.

Duffey, Betsy. *The Gadget War*. New York: Viking Press, 1991.

Erlbach, Arlene. *Bicycles*. Minneapolis: Lerner Publications, 1994.

Garrison, Webb. *Why Didn't I Think of That?: From Alarm Clocks to Zippers*. Englewood Cliffs, NJ: Prentice-Hall, 1977.

Gibbons, Gail. *Clocks and How They Go*. New York: Crowell, 1979.

Glover, David. *Pulleys and Gears*, 2nd edition. Portsmouth N.H.: Heinemann, 2006.

Graham, Ian. *Cars, Bikes, Trains, and Other Land Machines*. New York: Kingfisher Books, 1993.

Lafferty, Peter. *Archimedes*. New York: Bookwright, 1991.

Peppe, Rodney. *The Mice and the Clockwork Bus*. New York: Lothrop, Lee & Shepard Books, 1987.

Richards, Jon. *Forces & Simple Machines*. Brookfield, CT: Copper Beech Books, 2000.

_____. *Trains*. Brookfield, CT: Copper Beech Books, 1998.

Sadler, Wendy. *Using Pulleys and Gears*. Chicago: Raintree, 2005.

Solway, Andrew. *Castle Under Siege!: Simple Machines*. Chicago: Raintree, 2007.

Thales, Sharon. *Pulleys to the Rescue*. Mankato, MN: Capstone Press, 2008.

Wells, Robert E. *How Do You Lift a Lion?* Morton Grove, IL: A. Whitman, 1996.

Woods, Michael, and Mary B. Woods. *Ancient Machines: From Wedges to Waterwheels*. Minneapolis: Lerner Publishing, 2007.

Websites

- <http://www.ed.uri.edu:80/SMART96/ ELEMSC/SMARTmachines/machine.html>

  Work is Simple with Simple Machines: Classroom activities for learning about and designing simple machines. With overviews, outcomes, standards and benchmarks, links, and further resources.

- <http://www.galaxy.net:80/~k12/ machines/>

  Marvelous Machines: For teachers and students examining simple machines and friction. Includes background information for teachers, teacher's notes, activities, materials list, and references.

- <http://www.cpo.com/>

  The Cambridge Physics Outlet Online: Click on "Free Teacher Resources" and then on "Instruction sheets" to find activities on ropes and pulleys, as well as gears and levers. The activities provide helpful diagrams and ideas for teaching these concepts.

- <http://www.stemnet.nf.ca/CITE/ dacta.htm>

  Student Activity Sheets and Teacher's Guides: This site offers enrichment activities about simple machines, using Lego. Features include: student sheets, teacher's guide (with an introduction), concepts, investigation, and possible student responses. Great ideas for students who want to know more.

- <http://www.phschool.com/atschool/ science_explorer/Motion/Student_Area/ SE_M_S_CHAP1_index.html>

  Science Explorer: Motion, Forces, and Energy includes Internet Activities, self-tests, extensive links to related topics, and more.

- <http://www.howstuffworks.com/>

  How Stuff Works: Type "pulleys" or "gears" in the search box to find a number of articles describing the details of these simple machines. A great resource with diagrams, pictures, and a wealth of information.

Introduction

Throughout this unit, students will broaden their understanding of structures and mechanisms by looking at two special kinds of wheels: pulleys and gears. One or more pulleys are used to move an object from one place to another. Gears can be used in combination to change speed and direction of movement. Students will design and build pulley systems and gear systems, and will explore the advantages of each type of system.

By the end of this unit, students will demonstrate an understanding of the characteristics of pulleys and gears, design and make pulley systems and gear systems, and investigate how motion is transferred from one system to another. They will identify ways in which different systems function, and identify appropriate criteria to be considered when designing and making such systems.

Science Vocabulary

Continue to use your science and technology word wall to display new vocabulary as it is introduced.

Throughout this unit, teachers should use, and encourage students to use, vocabulary such as: *direction, speed, force, pulley, simple pulley, compound pulley, block and tackle, gear, spur gear, idle gear, crown gear, bevel gear, worm gear,* and *gear train.*

Note: Definitions and background information for these terms are provided in the related lesson.

Materials Required for the Unit

Classroom: pencils, string, clipboards, Plasticine, scissors, paint, paintbrushes, chart paper, markers, glue, tape, index cards, mural paper, stapler, overhead projector

Books, Pictures, and Illustrations: *The Bridge From A-Z* (book by Kathy Creaghan Gray), legends of Archimedes (two good sources are *Archimedes* by D.C. Ipsen and *Archimedes* by Sydney Gordon), version of *Rapunzel*, picture of drawbridge (included), "Ferris Wheel" (a short story by Webb Garrison in *Why Didn't I Think of That?*), "Origin of the Ferris Wheel" information sheet (included) diagram of a corkscrew (included)

Household: paper cups, empty thread spools

Equipment: spring scales, single pulleys, compound pulleys, weight set, commercially produced gear kits,

Other: access to a flagpole (with a manual pulley system), corrugated tubes, plastic pails with handles, heavy objects to fill pails (e.g., books, sand), rope, broom handles, long wooden board, screw hooks, various-sized boxes (e.g., milk cartons), nails, bicycle, guitar, straight pins, large corks, wagon, corrugated cardboard, empty cans, screw, screwdriver, pieces of wooden board (30 cm x 15 cm), hammer, nails, string, access to a strong horizontal bar, globe, toy car, metal washer, wooden blocks, double-handed corkscrews, bottle with cork inserted, assortment of spools

Note: This unit relies heavily on access to a variety of commercially produced kits of pulleys and gears. These kits usually include a variety of pulleys and gears, as well as activity cards or project booklets for construction. It is necessary to have sufficient quantities of these materials so that all students can construct pulley and gear systems in group settings. Most educational supply catalogues offer several options for construction kits of pulleys and gears. Teachers should review such catalogues in order to select kits appropriate to their classroom needs.

In addition to the commercially produced pulleys and gears used throughout the lessons in this unit, there are also several extension or activity centre suggestions for constructing pulleys and gears from everyday materials. These activities require a significant amount of pre-planning, gathering of materials, and construction.

A Note About Materials

The materials needed to complete some activities are extensive. Teachers should review the materials lists for the unit ahead of time and make a note of items that students may be able to bring from home (for example, plastic containers, paper plates and/or cups, spoons, pie plates, fabric samples, balls of wool). Then, prior to beginning the lesson, teachers can send a letter home with students asking parents/ guardians to donate some of these materials.

A Note About Safety

During their exploration of pulleys and gears, students should be able to identify, and understand, the importance of practices that ensure their safety and the safety of others. This includes knowing why long hair should be tied back and loose jewellery removed when working with pulleys and gears. Students also need to ensure pulleys and gears are securely fastened before testing them with a load.

1 Single Pulleys

Expectations

- **1.1** Assess the impact of pulley systems and gear systems on daily life

- **2.2** Use scientific inquiry/experimentation skills to investigate changes in force, distance, speed, and direction in pulley and gear systems

- **2.4** Use appropriate science and technology vocabulary, including *pulley, gear, force*, and *speed*, in oral and written communication

- **2.5** Use a variety of forms to communicate with different audiences and for a variety of purposes

- **3.1** Describe the purposes of pulley systems and gear systems

- **3.6** Identify pulley systems and gear systems that are used in daily life, and explain the purpose and basic operation of each

Science Background Information for Teachers

A variation of a wheel, a *pulley* is a machine. A rope or cable passes back and forth over one or more grooved wheels. One end of the rope is attached to the load, and the other end is pulled in order to move or lift the load. A *simple pulley* has only one wheel. This pulley changes the direction of a force but does not magnify the force. The pulley makes the task more convenient, because it is easier to pull a rope down than it is to lift a weight up. Single, fixed pulleys add no mechanical advantage to lifting a load, but do change the direction of applied force, which is useful if the load is in an inconvenient spot.

Materials

- access to a flagpole with a manual pulley system
- several plastic pails with handles
- heavy objects such as books or sand (to fill the pails)
- rope
- access to a strong, horizontal bar
- *The Bridge From A–Z*, a book by Kathy Creaghan Gray
- wagon

Activity

Take students outdoors to view a flagpole with a manual pulley system. If possible, ask your school custodian to show students how the pulley system works. After students have had an opportunity to observe the system in action, introduce the term *pulley*. Explain to students that a pulley is a wheel over which a rope or cable attached to a load is pulled to lift the load. Discuss the difficulties in raising a flag if a pulley system is not used.

Following this introduction to pulleys, fill several pails with heavy objects such as books or sand. Take students outside, using the wagon to transport the heavy pails with you. Locate a horizontal bar such as the kind found on a soccer goal or playground structure. Have students lift the pails, and discuss the difficulty of raising the load.

Safety Note: Take this opportunity to teach students that the proper way to lift a load is by bending the knees first so that the back is not strained.

Challenge students to determine a way of using a pulley to raise the pails. Throw a strong rope over the horizontal bar, and tie one end of the rope to the handle of a pail. Give students several opportunities to use the pulley to lift the pails and compare their efforts to those used to lift the pails by hand.

Back in the classroom, read aloud the book *The Bridge From A–Z*. The book is about the building of the longest bridge in the world over ice-covered water, linking Prince Edward Island and New Brunswick. Ask students:

- Were any pulleys used to build the bridge?
- How does a crane work?
- Does a crane use pulleys?
- How many elephants, hippopotamuses, and rhinoceroses could the floating Svanen crane hold at the same time? (500, 600, and 1 000)

Now, have students use their experiences with the flagpole, ropes, and buckets, and what they learned from the book to complete Activity Sheet A (2.1.1).

Activity Sheet A

Directions to students:

Draw a diagram of the pulley system you constructed to lift the pail. Label your diagram. Answer the questions to show what you have learned about pulleys (2.1.1).

Activity Centre

Give students ample opportunities to explore pulleys independently. Provide a variety of commercially produced pulleys, string, weight sets, and spring scales. Have students construct single pulley systems and use a spring scale to measure the loads lifted. To measure a load, have students attach it to one side of the pulley, and hook the spring scale to the other side. Pull down on the spring scale, and measure the mass being lifted.

Extensions

- Have students make their own single pulleys from everyday materials (or make models to further demonstrate the action and work that pulleys do). The following materials are required to make a single pulley: wax washer (cut a candle into slices, and drill a hole through the middle of one of the slices), nail, hammer, 6 metal washers (same size),

2 paper clips, empty thread spool, thin string, piece of wood (2 x 4 cut into 30-cm pieces).

1. Place the nail through the centre of the spool.
2. Place the wax washer between a piece of wood and the spool.
3. Use the hammer to nail the spool in place on the wood. Make sure the spool will turn freely.
4. Have one student hold the wood block vertically while another hangs a piece of string over the spool.
5. Tie each end of the string to a paper clip, and bend part of each paper clip so it becomes a hook.
6. Place a metal washer on each hook.

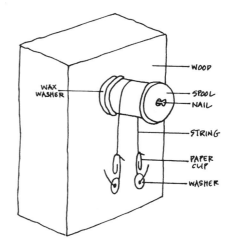

Give students time to explore the pulley and determine how it works to lift loads. Use the following instructions and questions to encourage exploration:

1. Remove the metal washer from one end of the pulley. How can you lift the washer on the other end without touching it?
2. When you lift the washer upward, in what direction do you pull the other end of the string?

▶

1

3. Hook three metal washers to one end of the pulley's string. Now, hook one washer to the other end of the pulley's string. Are the forces on each side of the pulley balanced? How could you balance the pulley?

■ Pulleys can be used to lift loads vertically, but they can also be used to move objects in a horizontal direction. Challenge students to design a way to use single pulleys to open and close curtains for a puppet show theatre. Use a large cardboard box for the stage, commercially produced pulleys, fabric for curtains, and other materials determined by students.

Single Fixed Pulley

Draw a labelled diagram of the pulley used to lift the heavy pail.

1. What is a pulley?

_____

_____

2. How does the pulley make work easier?

_____

_____

3. Where else are pulleys used?

_____

_____

Portage & Main Press, 2008, Hands-on Science & Technology, Grade 4, BLM, ISBN: 978-1-55379-179-9

2 | Compound Pulleys

Expectations

- **1.1** Assess the impact of pulley systems and gear systems on daily life

- **2.2** Use scientific inquiry/experimentation skills to investigate changes in force, distance, speed, and direction in pulley and gear systems

- **2.4** Use appropriate science and technology vocabulary, including *pulley, gear, force*, and *speed*, in oral and written communication

- **2.5** Use a variety of forms to communicate with different audiences and for a variety of purposes

- **3.1** Describe the purposes of pulley systems and gear systems

- **3.6** Identify pulley systems and gear systems that are used in daily life, and explain the purpose and basic operation of each

Science Background Information for Teachers

A *compound pulley* is a system that uses more than one pulley to lift or move loads. The more pulleys in the system, the greater the mechanical advantage the system offers.

A *block and tackle* (see diagram to right) is an example of a compound pulley. This system of pulleys and ropes reduces the effort required to lift or lower objects. One set of pulleys is fixed (to a ceiling, for example) and the second set of pulleys moves up and down freely with the load. The block and tackle is used on construction sites to lift heavy objects and in automobile service stations to lift engines. It is also commonly used to raise or lower a piano from a building.

In the block and tackle, more than one pulley is used.

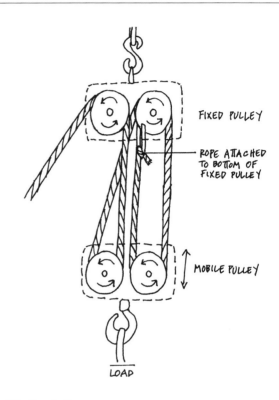

FIXED PULLEY

ROPE ATTACHED TO BOTTOM OF FIXED PULLEY

MOBILE PULLEY

LOAD

Materials

- 2 broom handles or hockey sticks
- long piece of rope (about 3 metres)
- legend of Archimedes (two good sources are: *Archimedes* by D. C. Ipsen and *Archimedes* by Sydney Gordon)

Note: One of the legends of Archimedes focuses on his use of a compound pulley. King Hieron of Syracuse challenged Archimedes to drag a large ship onto the beach by himself. Archimedes studied the problem and decided to use a simple machine, the pulley. He used a compound pulley attached to the ship, and he was able to drag the ship onto the shore.

Keep in mind that this is a legend. Although the science of using pulleys is accurate, it is unlikely that one would actually be able to accomplish this feat.

▶

Activity

Read aloud the legend of Archimedes, then discuss the pulley system Archimedes used to drag the ship ashore.

Note: In the legend, Archimedes is able to drag the ship ashore because of the pulley system he devised, made of two wheels, which produced a mechanical advantage of two. That is, he could move twice the load that he would have been able to move without the pulley system, with the same effort. The more wheels in a pulley system, the less effort that is required.

Explain to students that they are going to have an opportunity to find out how a compound pulley works. Have two students hold the two broomsticks in a vertical position, about 30 centimetres apart. Challenge other students, one at a time, to try to pull the sticks together, while the two students try to keep the sticks apart. As a group, discuss the difficulty of moving the broomsticks together. Now, challenge students to find a way to use rope to pull the broomsticks together. Allow plenty of time for discussion and experimentation.

Note: While they are experimenting, be sure that students are careful not to get their hands stuck between the broomsticks as the sticks are being pulled together.

To accomplish the task, tie one end of the rope around the end of one of the broomsticks. Then, loop the rope around the two broomsticks (as shown in the diagram to the right). As the rope is pulled, the broomsticks will be forced together.

Following the investigation, discuss the activity. Explain to students that they constructed a type of compound pulley system. The two sticks acted like wheels on the pulley. Introduce the term *block and tackle* as the system used to pull the sticks together.

Ask:

- Without the block and tackle, was it difficult to pull the sticks together? Why?
- How did the block and tackle make it easier to pull the sticks together?

Note: Each time the rope is looped around the two sticks, the pulling power increases (in theory the pulling power doubles). Friction will decrease some of the pulling power. The disadvantage is that if your pulling power doubles so does the distance you have to pull the rope.

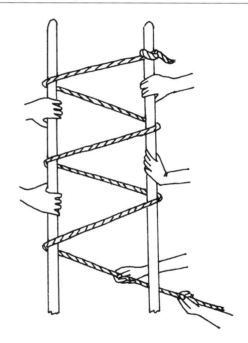

Activity Sheet A

Directions to students:

Describe your investigation with a block and tackle pulley. Answer the questions on the activity sheet (2.2.1).

Activity Centre

Have students design and construct a clothesline to see, firsthand, a practical application of pulley systems. Provide

▶

commercially produced pulleys (or use the model pulleys constructed in the extension activity in lesson 1) a hammer, 2 nails, string, a 2-metre board, a piece of paper, and a paper clip. Nail the two pulleys to opposite ends of the board. Attach the string between the two pulleys, and tie it so you have a continuous loop over both pulleys. Hook the paper clip to the string.

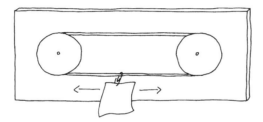

Have students attach the paper to the paper clip on the clothesline and move it along the line. Students can also make paper clothing to attach and move along the clothesline.

Note: This pulley system is similar to those used on ski lifts to move skiers both horizontally and vertically up and down a mountain.

Extensions

■ Discuss and compare single pulleys and block and tackle pulleys. Have students fold a large sheet of paper in half and label the sections with the names of these two types of pulleys. Encourage them to draw labelled diagrams and provide written descriptions of each type of pulley.

■ Invite a guest speaker from a car service centre, a construction company, or a piano moving company to explain and demonstrate how a real block and tackle pulley system works.

Compound Pulley

Draw a diagram, and describe how you were able to pull the two broomsticks together.

```
┌─────────────────────────────────────────────────────────┐
│                                                           │
│                                                           │
│                                                           │
│                                                           │
│                                                           │
│                                                           │
│                                                           │
│                                                           │
│                                                           │
└─────────────────────────────────────────────────────────┘
```

_____

_____

_____

1. How were the rope and broomsticks similar to a pulley system?

_____

_____

2. What type of pulley system was shown in this activity?

_____

_____

3. How is the compound pulley different from a single pulley?

_____

_____

Portage & Main Press, 2008, Hands-on Science & Technology, Grade 4, BLM, ISBN: 978-1-55379-179-9

3 | Comparing Pulleys

Expectations

- **2.2** Use scientific inquiry/experimentation skills to investigate changes in force, distance, speed, and direction in pulley and gear systems

- **2.4** Use appropriate science and technology vocabulary, including *pulley, gear, force*, and *speed*, in oral and written communication

- **2.5** Use a variety of forms to communicate with different audiences and for a variety of purposes

- **3.5** Distinguish between pulley systems and gear systems that increase force and those that increase speed

Note: Prior to the lesson, construct both a single pulley and a compound pulley to use for discussion, comparison, and demonstration. Instructions and diagrams are provided (2.3.1). This lesson is best taught as a large-group activity.

Materials

- board (long enough to span across desks, tables, chart stands, or ladders)
- screw hooks
- paper cups
- pencils
- string
- single pulley
- weight sets measuring grams and multiples of grams
- spring scales (that measure grams)
- compound pulley

Activity

Prior to the activity, position a board so that it spans a distance of at least a metre (use chairs, tables, or taller props such as ladders or chart stands so that you do not have to crouch in order to use the pulleys).

Screw two screw hooks into the board (several centimetres from each end). Hook the two pulleys onto the screw hooks.

As a class, discuss pulleys and how they are useful. Ask:

- What is a pulley?
- What types of pulleys have you investigated?
- How are pulleys used?
- How do pulleys make work easier?

Explain to students that they will be comparing two different types of pulleys. Display the single pulley and compound pulley for students to examine and manipulate. Ask:

- How are these pulleys the same?
- How are they different?
- How do you think they compare in their abilities to lift a load?

Provide students with Activity Sheet A (2.3.2). Have students identify and record the names of the two types of pulleys on their activity sheets.

Determine the weight to be placed on the single fixed pulley, and have a student place the weight in a paper cup. Hook the spring scale onto the other end of the string. Explain to students that by pulling down on the spring scale, the load can be lifted. The scale will show the amount of force needed to lift the load in the cup. Ask:

- If you lift the load by pulling down on the spring scale, how much force do you think you will use?

Have students share their estimates and record them on their activity sheets, then test their predictions and record the results.

Repeat the same procedure with the compound pulley, and record estimates and results. Ask:

- How did the pulleys compare for lifting the load?

- Was the same amount of force required for both pulleys to lift the load?
- Which pulley required less force to lift the load?

Repeat the same procedure, using different weights on both pulleys.

After students complete their activity sheets, discuss their responses as a class.

Activity Sheet A

Note: This activity sheet is to be completed during the lesson.

Directions to students:

Test each pulley, and record the results on the chart. Look over the results, and answer the questions (2.3.2).

Activity Centre

Provide an opportunity for students to explore pulley systems independently. Attach a fixed pulley to the ceiling so students have plenty of space to experiment. Provide additional pulleys, string, weights, and spring scales. Have students construct and compare pulley systems with different numbers of pulleys, as in the diagram to the right.

Have students record results on the activity centre sheet provided (2.3.3).

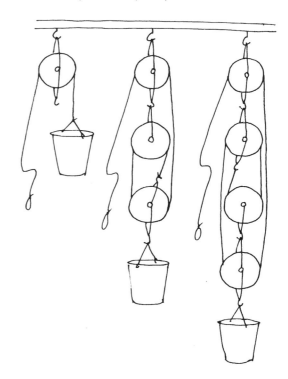

Assessment Suggestion

Observe students at the activity centre as they construct, test, and compare their pulleys. Focus on their abilities to follow directions, then measure and record results accurately. Use the Anecdotal Record sheet, found on page 19, to record results.

Instructions for Constructing Pulleys

Single Pulley — Pulley #1

1. With a pencil, punch two holes in a paper cup on opposite sides of the rim. Tie a string through the holes to make a handle.

2. Thread the string over a pulley.

3. Tie a loop at the end of the loose string so it can be hooked onto the spring scale.

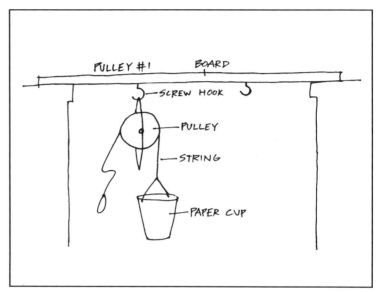

Compound Pulley — Pulley #2

1. Use a pencil to punch two holes in a paper cup on opposite sides of the rim. Tie a string through the holes to make a handle.

2. Thread the string over a pulley.

3. Take the other end of the string, and pass it around a second pulley, then attach it to the fixed pulley.

4. Hook the paper cup onto the hook of the bottom pulley.

5. Tie a loop at the end of the loose string so it can be hooked onto the spring scale.

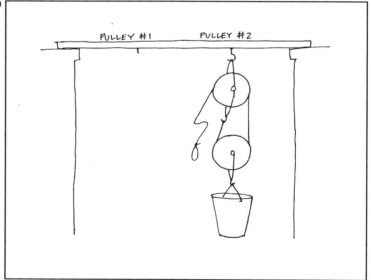

Portage & Main Press, 2008, Hands-on Science & Technology, Grade 4, BLM. ISBN: 978-1-55379-179-9

Comparing Pulleys

What type of pulley is Pulley #1? _____

What type of pulley is Pulley #2? _____

Single Fixed Pulley Weight to be Lifted (g)	Force (g)		Compound Pulley Weight to be Lifted (g)	Force (g)	
	Estimate	Result		Estimate	Result

1. Which pulley made the loads easiest to lift?

_____

2. What did the spring scale measure?

_____

_____

3. How does the use of the spring scale help you to compare pulleys?

_____

_____

4. What did you learn about single and compound pulleys?

_____

_____

_____

Portage & Main Press, 2008, Hands-on Science & Technology, Grade 4, BLM, ISBN: 978-1-55379-179-9

Comparing Pulleys

Pulley System/ Number of Pulleys	Weight to be Lifted (g)	Force (g)	
		Estimate	Result

Portage & Main Press, 2008, Hands-on Science & Technology, Grade 4, BLM, ISBN: 978-1-55379-179-9

Activity Centre

4 Gears

Expectations

- **2.3** Use technological problem-solving skills to design, build, and test a pulley or gear system that performs a specific task

- **2.4** Use appropriate science and technology vocabulary, including *pulley, gear, force*, and *speed*, in oral and written communication

- **2.5** Use a variety of forms to communicate with different audiences and for a variety of purposes

- **3.1** Describe the purposes of pulley systems and gear systems

- **3.4** Describe, using students' observations, how gears operate in one plane and in two planes

- **3.6** Identify pulley systems and gear systems that are used in daily life, and explain the purpose and basic operation of each

- **3.7** Explain how the gear system on a bicycle works

Science Background Information for Teachers

Gears are wheels that fit together to create movement. A gear is a wheel with cogs, or teeth, around it. As a gear turns, its teeth mesh, or lock, with chains or the teeth on other gears. When the teeth of a turning gear mesh with the teeth of a second gear, the second gear is turned in the direction opposite to that of the first gear. Gears are used to change the speed, or the direction, of the movement. A gear is a modified wheel that sends turning motion and power from one part of a machine to another. Gear size determines the turning speed. Large gears spin more slowly than small gears, allowing machine parts to operate at different speeds.

Materials

- bicycle (more than one speed)
- chart paper
- markers
- commercially produced gear kits
- corrugated cardboard (with one side of corrugation exposed)
- 3 clean, empty cans, tops removed, (shallow cans of different size diameters work best, such as those from tuna, salmon, cat food, and so on)
- screws
- screwdriver
- pieces of wooden board about 30 cm x 15 cm
- glue or tape
- hammer
- nails
- scissors

Activity: Part One

Have students examine the bicycle. In their own words, have them identify the various parts of the bike and explain how the parts work together to make the bike move. Record their ideas on chart paper. To encourage discussion, ask:

- What do you do with the pedals?
- What happens when you push on the pedals? What other parts of the bike are put into motion?

Discuss with and demonstrate to students that the pedals are the "input component," and the rear wheel is the "output component" on a bicycle.

To continue the discussion, ask:

- Where are the gears located on the bike?
- What do the gears look like?
- How do the gears fit together to create movement?

- How many gears do you see?
- What do the gears do? How do they work?
- What does it mean to *change gears* when you are riding a bike?
- What happens when you change gears?
- Why are the gears on a bike sometimes greased or oiled?

As a group, investigate how the gears work and change. If space permits, demonstrate how to change gears while riding the bike (this can be done outdoors, in the gym, or in a hallway).

Following this discussion and demonstration, divide the class into working groups, and provide each group with a commercially produced gear kit. Provide plenty of time for free exploration with the materials, then give students Activity Sheet A (2.4.1) to record their discoveries and observations.

Activity Sheet A

Directions to students:

Experiment with your gears, using the activity sheet as a guide (2.4.1).

Activity: Part Two

As a class, construct a model gear system, using everyday materials:

Cut strips of the corrugated cardboard, and wrap the strips around the three cans so the corrugated side of the cardboard is on the outside of the cans. Secure the ends with tape

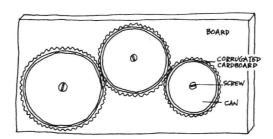

or glue. Use a hammer and a nail to make a hole at the bottom of each can. Attach the cans to a wooden board with screws. Make sure each can touches the can(s) next to it and the corrugated cardboard meshes.

Give students time to manipulate the gear system and observe how each gear moves. Provide the following guidance:

1. Turn the first can clockwise. What happens to the second can? What happens to the third can?
2. Use a marker to mark one of the gear teeth on each can. Now, count the gear teeth on each can.
3. Turn the largest can. How many turns does the smallest can make when the largest can turns once around?

Activity: Part Three

Place a sheet of corrugated cardboard on a table with the corrugated side facing up. Have students place one of the can gears wrapped in corrugated cardboard (from Activty: Part Two) on the sheet of cardboard.

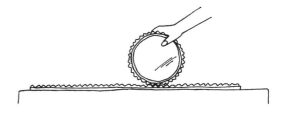

Have two students hold the cardboard still while another student slowly turns the can. Ask:

- What happens?
- What would happen if the cardboard was on an incline?
- Would the can be able to travel up or down?

4

After students have tried to move the can on an incline, explain that many trains use the gear system to climb steep mountain slopes. Students may want to try to find out more about these trains and report back to the class.

Activity: Part Four

As a class, assess the environmental impact of people riding bicycles instead of driving cars. Although gears on a bicycle reduce the effort needed to pedal it, a person exerts more energy riding a bicycle than driving (or being a passenger in) a car. In addition, it usually takes longer to arrive at a destination by bicycle than it does by car. However, the bicycle is much more environmentally friendly than a car, because it does not use fossil fuel to power it.

Distribute a copy of Activity Sheet B (2.4.2) to each student, and have students write a persuasive text to support their views on the topic.

Activity Sheet B

Directions to students:

Describe the advantages and disadvantages of using bicycles and cars for travel. State your opinion on the environmental impact of using bicycles instead of cars.

Activity: Part Five

Take a field trip to a museum that has a windmill. Explain to students that the wind turns the large sails or sweeps of a windmill, which are connected to drive shafts by large wooden cogs.

Take another field trip to see a watermill in use. Explain to students how the water is trapped behind a dam and released along a stream. The water pours over the blades of a waterwheel to make them turn.

Note: In both the windmill and watermill, water or wind power is used to turn a shaft with gears attached. Using different gears to change the speed and direction allows the shafts to turn wheels and turbines to produce electricity or to drive machinery. Typically, in old windmills the gears will turn the grindstone to grind seed into flour.

Activity Centre

At the activity centre, provide bottle caps (with ridges on the edges), hammers, nails, and pieces of wood (approximately 20 cm x 8 cm). Have students construct a gear chain: Have an adult hammer nails through two bottle caps side by side onto the block of wood. Make sure the ridges on the caps face up and fit into each other. Have students experiment with the gears. Give the following instructions:

1. Turn one cap. What happens to the other cap?
2. Add a third bottle cap to the gear chain, and experiment with the movement.
3. Predict what direction a fourth cap will turn, a fifth cap, and a sixth cap.
4. Attach the fourth, fifth, and sixth bottle caps to the gear chain, and test your predictions.

Date: _____   Name: _____

Experimenting With Gears

1. What are the important features of a gear?_____

_____

2. Put two gears together so that the teeth mesh. Turn the first gear clockwise. What happens to the second gear?

_____

3. Draw a diagram to show how turning the first gear affects the second gear. Be sure to include arrows to show the direction that each gear turns.

4. Put a large gear and a small gear together so that the teeth mesh. Turn the large gear once around completely. How many turns does the small gear make?

_____

5. What else have you learned about gears?_____

_____

_____

Portage & Main Press, 2008, Hands-on Science & Technology, Grade 4, BLM, ISBN: 978-1-55379-179-9

4A

Using Bicycles or Cars for Travel

Advantages of Using Bicycles	
Disadvantages of Using Bicycles	
Advantages of Using Cars	
Disadvantages of Using Cars	

How do you think using bicycles instead of cars would affect the environment?

_____

_____

_____

_____

_____

_____

_____

_____

Portage & Main Press, 2008, Hands-on Science & Technology, Grade 4, BLM, ISBN: 978-1-55379-179-9

5 Gears and Direction of Movement

Expectations

- **2.2** Use scientific inquiry/experimentation skills to investigate changes in force, distance, speed, and direction in pulley and gear systems

- **2.3** Use technological problem-solving skills to design, build, and test a pulley or gear system that performs a specific task

- **2.4** Use appropriate science and technology vocabulary, including *pulley, gear, force*, and *speed*, in oral and written communication

- **2.5** Use a variety of forms to communicate with different audiences and for a variety of purposes

- **3.1** Describe the purposes of pulley systems and gear systems

- **3.4** Describe, using students' observations, how gears operate in one plane and in two planes

Science Background Information for Teachers

There are several different kinds of gears. As well, gears operate in one plane (for example, spur gears, idle gears) and in two planes (for example, crown gears, bevel gears, worm gears). These are some examples of gears:

Spur gear: Consists of two interlocking toothed wheels in the same plane, such as those found on a manual can opener. The wheels turn in opposite directions.

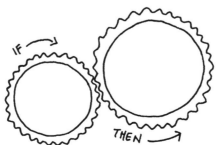

Idle gear: If the rotation of the wheels of a spur gear is needed to go in the same direction, an idle gear is placed between the two toothed wheels.

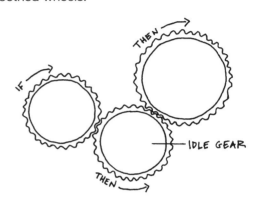

Crown gear: Found in the rear end of a rear-wheel drive car or the front end of a front-wheel drive car. It allows the powered wheels to rotate at different speeds when turning a corner.

Bevel gear: Consists of two toothed wheels that are bevelled and meshed at an angle, altering the direction of the rotation.

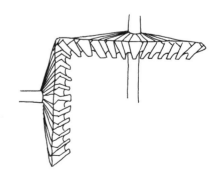

Worm gear: Consists of one circular gear with teeth and a screw-like tube on the other gear. This type of gear is found on the tuning pegs of a guitar or violin.

Note: It may be beneficial to students to create a bulletin board display featuring different types gears. The display can include drawings, pictures of useful objects that contain gears, terms printed on index cards, and definitions written in student language. This type of display will help to solidify students' understanding of the concepts being focused on.

Materials

- guitar
- straight pins (or finishing nails)
- large corks

Activity

As a class, review the gears that were made in the previous lesson. Focus on how they work to create movement. To demonstrate how the gears worked together on one plane or flat surface, use one of the models made by students. Explain to students that they are going to make gears that will change the direction of the force or movement.

Divide the class into working groups, and provide each group with two corks and several straight pins. Give the groups the following directions, while demonstrating the steps:

1. Stick 8 or 10 straight pins in a circle around the top rim of a cork. The pins must be spaced at equal distance from one another. Repeat step 1 on the second cork.

2. Place one cork on a table, with the pins facing upward. Hold the second cork at a right angle to the first cork so that the pins mesh together like the teeth of gears (see below).

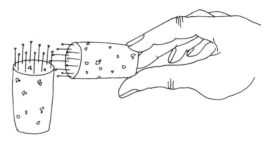

3. Slowly turn the cork that is in your hand, and observe what happens to the cork on the table. As the groups are investigating this model, explain to students that they have discovered how a worm gear, bevel gear, and crown gear work.

Tell students that the most common type of worm gear is the metal tuning peg found on a guitar. Show students the guitar, and demonstrate the peg. Turning the peg in one direction will tighten the string, producing a higher pitch, while turning the peg in the opposite direction will loosen the string, producing a lower pitch. Allow students opportunities to manipulate the pegs on the guitar and examine the gears. Explain that the worm gear is often used to change the direction of movement, just as it did with the corks.

▶

5

Activity Sheet A

Directions to students:

Draw a diagram of your pin gears, and explain how the gears work together. Now, draw a diagram of the gears on the guitar. Answer the questions about this type of gear (2.5.1).

Activity Centre

Provide a variety of objects that contain gears, such as manual and electric can openers, hand-held food grinders, hand mixers, hand drills, music boxes, old watches and clocks, windup alarm clocks, and windup toys. Encourage students to look for items at home that contain gears and bring them to class for display and investigation. Have students observe the number and types of gears that are used in each object. Challenge them to sort the items according to the types of gears used in each.

Note: You may wish to divide this centre into two sections: one where students can actually take apart items such as old clocks and watches; the other where students examine the items without disassembling them.

Gears and Directional Movement

1. Draw a diagram of your pin gears, and explain how they work.

_____

_____

_____

2. Draw a diagram of the gears on the guitar peg.

For what are the gears on the guitar peg used? How do they work?

_____

_____

_____

5A

Portage & Main Press, 2008, Hands-on Science & Technology, Grade 4, BLM, ISBN: 978-1-55379-179-9

6 | Designing and Constructing With Gears

Expectations

- **2.3** Use technological problem-solving skills to design, build, and test a pulley or gear system that performs a specific task

- **2.4** Use appropriate science and technology vocabulary, including *pulley, gear, force*, and *speed*, in oral and written communication

- **2.5** Use a variety of forms to communicate with different audiences and for a variety of purposes

Materials

- chart paper
- markers
- commercially produced gear kits
- other materials as identified by students for constructing an object with working gears

Activity

As a class, brainstorm a list of items that have gears as part of their working mechanisms. Record students' responses on chart paper. Now, challenge students to think of objects or toys with gears that they could design and construct. Refer to objects that they have examined, as well as to their own creative ideas.

Note: Many commercially produced gear kits come with plans for several projects. Students can refer to these for ideas and modify designs as they see fit.

Divide the class into working groups, and provide the groups with gears, materials, as well as any resources that may assist them as they plan, design, and construct their object. Also, provide Activity Sheet A (2.6.1) for students to use as a guide and follow-up.

Once the groups have constructed and tested their models, have them present their projects to the class.

Activity Sheet A

Note: This is a two-page activity sheet.

Directions to students:

Draw diagrams of your design and finished product, and answer the questions (2.6.1).

Extension

Challenge students to use gears to make clocks with moving hands. They can use commercially produced gears, as well as gears made from everyday materials.The challenges may include:

- a clock with two hands that move clockwise
- a clock with hands that move counterclockwise
- a clock with an hour hand that goes backward and a minute hand that goes forward
- a clock with a minute hand that goes two times faster than the hour hand

Assessment Suggestions

- As a class, develop criteria for the gear system construction project. These may include the following:
    - accurate list of materials
    - modifications to original design
    - working final product
    - clear oral presentation

  List these criteria on the Rubric sheet, found on page 23, and record results for each group.

- Have students complete a Student Self-Assessment sheet, found on page 26, to reflect on what they have learned about gears.

Design and Construct With Gears

1. Our group will make a _____

that uses gears for movement.

2. Our design:

```
┌─────────────────────────────────────────────┐
│                                               │
│                                               │
│                                               │
│                                               │
│                                               │
│                                               │
│                                               │
│                                               │
│                                               │
│                                               │
│                                               │
│                                               │
│                                               │
│                                               │
│                                               │
│                                               │
└─────────────────────────────────────────────┘
```

3. Materials required:

_____   _____   _____

_____   _____   _____

_____   _____   _____

Portage & Main Press, 2008, Hands-on Science & Technology, Grade 4, BLM, ISBN: 978-1-55379-179-9

4. We have constructed and tested our model. These are the modifications we made to our original design: _____

_____

_____

5. Here is a labelled diagram of our final product:

[ ]

6. This is how our product uses gears for movement:

_____

_____

_____

_____

Portage & Main Press, 2008, Hands-on Science & Technology, Grade 4, BLM, ISBN: 978-1-55379-179-9

7 | Motion

Expectations

- **2.4** Use appropriate science and technology vocabulary, including *pulley, gear, force*, and *speed*, in oral and written communication

- **2.5** Use a variety of forms to communicate with different audiences and for a variety of purposes

- **3.2** Describe how rotary motion in one system or its components is transferred to another system or component in the same structure

Science Background Information for Teachers

Motion is the process of changing place or position. Four types of motion are:

Linear: Motion in a direct path, such as a sliding door or a nail being driven into a piece of wood

Rotational: Motion of turning on an axis, such as wheels, gears, Ferris wheels, and Earth

Reciprocating: Motion of an up-and-down nature in which the object returns to its original position, such as in a stapler or a self-inking stamp. Reciprocating engines produce this motion of pistons in cylinders.

Oscillating: Motion of a back-and-forth nature from a given fixed point, such as a swing, pendulum, or oscillating fan

Materials

- index cards
- markers
- chart paper
- "Ferris Wheel," a short story by Webb Garrison, in *Why Didn't I Think of That?*
- globe
- overhead projector
- "Origin of the Ferris Wheel" information sheet (included. Make an overhead copy of this sheet.) (2.7.1)
- toy car
- mural paper
- stapler
- pendulum (tie a washer to the end of a piece of string)

Activity: Part One

Provide students with index cards and markers. Have them title their cards "Motion," then, in their own words, write a definition for the term *motion* on the card.

As students share their definitions with the class, record their ideas on chart paper. Ask:

- In what different ways can objects move?

On chart paper, record examples of things that move (for example, cars, bikes, balls, swings, humans, Earth). Read aloud the short story "Ferris Wheel," or the information sheet. Ask:

- How many of you have gone for a ride on a Ferris wheel?
- What type of motion does a Ferris wheel have?
- How is this motion produced? (by a wheel turning on an axis)

Discuss the term *rotational motion*. Display the globe, and have students spin it to observe the rotational motion of the globe on its axis. As a class, determine a definition for this type of motion, and record the definition on chart paper. Brainstorm examples of rotational motion, and include these on the anchor chart. Ask:

- What other types of motion can you think of?

Students will likely have their own terms for linear motion (such as "moving forward" or "moving backward"). As they present their descriptions, introduce the term *linear motion*.

▶

Use the toy car to demonstrate this type of motion. As a class, determine a definition for this term, and record it on the anchor chart. Include examples with the definition.

Now, have students think of other ways that objects move. Display the stapler, and ask:

■ How does the stapler move?
■ How is the movement different from rotational motion?
■ How is its movement different from linear motion?

Introduce the term *reciprocating motion*. As a class, define this term, and record the definition on chart paper. Encourage students to provide examples of reciprocating motion. Record these on the anchor chart.

Display the pendulum for students to examine. Have students describe the type of motion they see as the pendulum swings back and forth. Introduce the term *oscillating motion*. Refer back to the Ferris wheel. Ask:

■ How do the seats on the Ferris wheel move? (the seats oscillate, or swing, back and forth)

Have students determine a definition and identify examples of oscillating motion. Record these on the anchor chart.

As a class, review the four types of motion presented in this activity. Divide the class into working groups. Provide each group with four copies of Activity Sheet A (2.7.2). Have students in each group work together to complete the activity sheets.

Activity Sheet A

Note: Four copies of the sheet are required for each working group.

Directions to students:

Record your ideas about each type of motion on a separate chart. Record the type of motion

in the top centre column. As a group, define the term. Provide examples and diagrams to show your understanding of this type of motion (2.7.2).

Activity: Part Two

As a class, create a concept web on a large sheet of mural paper. Title the web "Motion" (as below).

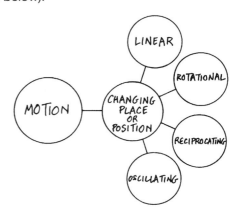

Note: Save the concept web, as well as the anchor chart developed in this lesson, for use in lesson 8.

Activity Centre

Provide several objects and pictures of devices that exemplify motion. For example:

linear: toy cars and airplanes, zippers

rotational: gears, pulleys, merry-go-rounds

reciprocating: self-inking stamps, click-top pens, doorbells

oscillating: pendulums, grandfather clocks, infant swings, cradles

Have students examine the objects and pictures and classify them according to the type of motion the object produces.

▶

7

Extension

Throughout the unit, encourage students to look for devices that move in each of the four ways discussed in this lesson. Invite them to add examples to the anchor charts and/or display devices at the activity centre.

Assessment Suggestion

Observe students as they work in groups to define, diagram, and give examples of the four types of motion. Use the Anecdotal Record sheet, found on page 19, to record your observations.

Origin of the Ferris Wheel

The Ferris wheel is named after George W. Ferris, a bridge builder from Pittsburgh, Pennsylvania. He built the Ferris wheel for the 1893 Chicago World's Fair. The organizers of the fair wanted something as spectacular as the Eiffel Tower, which had been built for the 1889 World's Fair in Paris.

The idea for the gigantic wheel came to Ferris in 1891 while he was at an engineer's luncheon. The guest speaker complained that the Chicago World's Fair was only two years away, and nothing had been found to rival the Eiffel Tower. As George Ferris listened, he reportedly scribbled a design of a great wheel on a napkin.

The Ferris wheel was an engineering wonder. The wheel, which stood as high as a 26-storey building, was 76 metres in diameter and had a circumference of 251 metres. Two steel towers, each 43 metres in height and connected by a 14-metre axle, supported the wheel. The axle was the largest single piece of forged steel ever made at the time. Thirty-six wooden cars, each with room to hold 60 people, were attached to the wheel.

Although the original Ferris wheel was destroyed in 1906, today Ferris wheels can be found throughout the world.

Portage & Main Press, 2008, Hands-on Science & Technology, Grade 4, BLM, ISBN: 978-1-55379-179-9

Date: _____

Names: _____

Motion

Definition	Type of Motion	Diagrams
	Examples	

Portage & Main Press, 2008, Hands-on Science & Technology, Grade 4, BLM, ISBN: 978-1-55379-179-9

8 | Changing Motion

Expectations

- **2.4** Use appropriate science and technology vocabulary, including *pulley, gear, force,* and *speed,* in oral and written communication

- **2.5** Use a variety of forms to communicate with different audiences and for a variety of purposes

- **3.2** Describe how rotary motion in one system or its components is transferred to another system or component in the same structure

- **3.3** Describe how one type of motion can be transformed into another type of motion using pulleys or gears

Science Background Information for Teachers

Some machines can change one type of motion to another type of motion. For example, a screw is turned through rotational movement but creates a linear movement through a piece of wood. A car engine also changes one type of motion to another. The pistons move in a reciprocating manner, which cause the wheels to turn in a rotational manner. This enables the car to move in a linear way.

Materials

- anchor chart(s) (from lesson 7)
- chart paper
- markers
- pictures of cars
- overhead projector
- screws
- screwdrivers
- wood blocks
- double-handled corkscrews
- bottle with cork in it
- diagram of corkscrew (included) (Make an overhead transparency of this sheet.) (2.8.1)
- concept web developed in lesson 7

Activity: Part One

Use the anchor chart(s) and definitions from the previous lesson to review the four types of motion (linear, rotational, reciprocating, and oscillating). Divide the class into working groups. Provide the groups with screws, screwdrivers, and blocks of wood. Have students use the screwdrivers to insert several screws into the pieces of wood. Ask:

- When you insert a screw into wood, what type of motion do you use as you move the screwdriver? (rotational)
- As the screw moves through the wood, what other type of motion occurs? (linear)
- How is a screw different from a nail?

Explain that, like the screw, some machines change one type of motion to another type of motion. Rotational motion was used to move the screw in a linear motion through the wood.

Distribute a copy of Activity Sheet A (2.8.2) to each student. Also, distribute the double-handled corkscrews for students to examine and manipulate. Have them draw a labelled diagram of the corkscrew on their activity sheets. Ask:

- What simple machines do you see in this corkscrew? (screw, gear, lever)
- How does this device change one type of motion to another?

Demonstrate how this machine removes a cork from a bottle (for safety purposes when working with a glass bottle, ensure that this is done by an adult only). Explain that the corkscrew uses both the screw and the rack and pinion to pull a cork from a bottle. A *rack and pinion* is a gear mechanism (the *rack* is a bar with teeth on it that meshes with a toothed gear called a *pinion*). The long handles with pinions produce considerable leverage on the rack. As the corkscrew is placed into the cork and screwed in, the handles rise. Once the screw is fully inserted, the handles are pushed down, so the pinions force up the rack, and the cork comes out of the bottle. This device, like the screw, changes rotational motion to linear motion. Display the diagram of the corkscrew (2.8.1), and encourage students to describe this process in their own words (using the diagram as a reference).

Activity: Part Two

Add to the concept web (from lesson 7) with ideas from this lesson. For example:

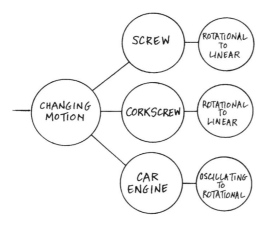

Activity Sheet A

Directions to students:

Draw a labelled diagram of the double-handled corkscrew. Describe how this machine works. Answer the question at the bottom of the page (2.8.2).

Corkscrew

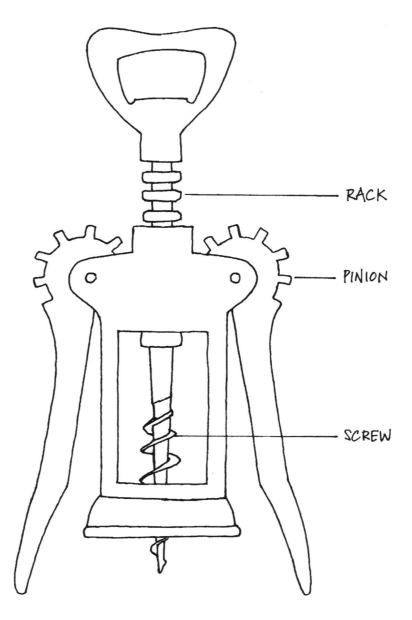

RACK

PINION

SCREW

1. **Screw is inserted into cork (rotational movement changes to linear movement).**

2. **Teeth on rack mesh with teeth on pinions.**

3. **Handles rise.**

4. **Force on handles removes cork.**

Portage & Main Press, 2008, Hands-on Science & Technology, Grade 4, BLM, ISBN: 978-1-55379-179-9

Changing Motion

1. Draw a labelled diagram of the corkscrew.

[ ]

2. Describe in detail how the corkscrew works to remove a cork from a bottle.

_____

_____

_____

_____

3. What is a rack and pinion?

_____

_____

_____

_____

Portage & Main Press, 2008, Hands-on Science & Technology, Grade 4, BLM, ISBN: 978-1-55379-179-9

9 Designing and Constructing a Pulley and Gear System

Expectations

- **2.3** Use technological problem-solving skills to design, build, and test a pulley or gear system that performs a specific task

- **2.4** Use appropriate science and technology vocabulary, including *pulley, gear, force*, and *speed*, in oral and written communication

- **2.5** Use a variety of forms to communicate with different audiences and for a variety of purposes

- **3.2** Describe how rotary motion in one system or its components is transferred to another system or component in the same structure

- **3.6** Identify pulley systems and gear systems that are used in daily life, and explain the purpose and basic operation of each

Materials

- version of the story *Rapunzel*
- Plasticine
- boxes of various sizes (milk cartons, cardboard tubes, and so on) (for building castles)
- scissors
- string
- assortment of spools
- nails
- pencils
- paint and paintbrushes (for decorating the castles)
- diagram of drawbridge design (included for teacher reference) (2.9.1)
- gears

Activity

Read the story *Rapunzel* to students. Ask:

- Can you think of ways to get into a castle or tower other than by climbing up Rapunzel's hair?
- How does a drawbridge work?
- Can you think of ways to use pulleys and gears to make a drawbridge work?
- What type of change in motion do gears and pulleys make?

Challenge students to build their own castles, with drawbridges that use a pulley system to work. Divide the class into working groups, and display the materials that students can use to build their castles. Emphasize that they need to include a drawbridge that uses pulleys and gears to be raised and lowered. The drawbridges need to be attached in a way that they can be lowered and raised. The illustration on page 132 (2.9.1) is an example of one of many possible solutions to this challenge.

Note: You may wish to discuss this illustration with students or make an actual model to show them. Either option will help them formulate ideas for their own drawbridge designs.

Provide each group with Activity Sheet A (2.9.2) on which students can plan and design their castles. Provide plenty of time for students to plan, draw diagrams, and list materials they will need. Once all groups have agreed on a plan, they can construct their castles and test their designs.

Following construction, have each group present its final project to their classmates.

▶

9

Activity Sheet A

Note: This is a two-page activity sheet.

Directions to students:

Use the activity sheet to help you plan, design, and test your castle and drawbridge (2.9.2).

Activity Centre

Provide a variety of materials, and allow students to be creative in constructing items that include pulley systems. These may include fishing rods, a clothesline-type pulley system for displaying student work in the classroom, toy cranes, flagpoles, sailboats with pulley systems to raise the sails, model ski lifts, as well as any ideas that students may have.

Commercially produced pulley kits usually include activity cards or project booklets with ideas on designing and constructing with pulleys. Allow students ample opportunities to use these materials to construct items with pulleys.

Assessment Suggestions

- As students work together to build their castles and drawbridges, observe their ability to work together as a group. Use the Cooperative Skills Teacher Assessment sheet, found on page 25, to record results.

- Have students complete a Cooperative Skills Self-Assessment sheet, found on page 27, to reflect on their own group work.

Drawbridge Design

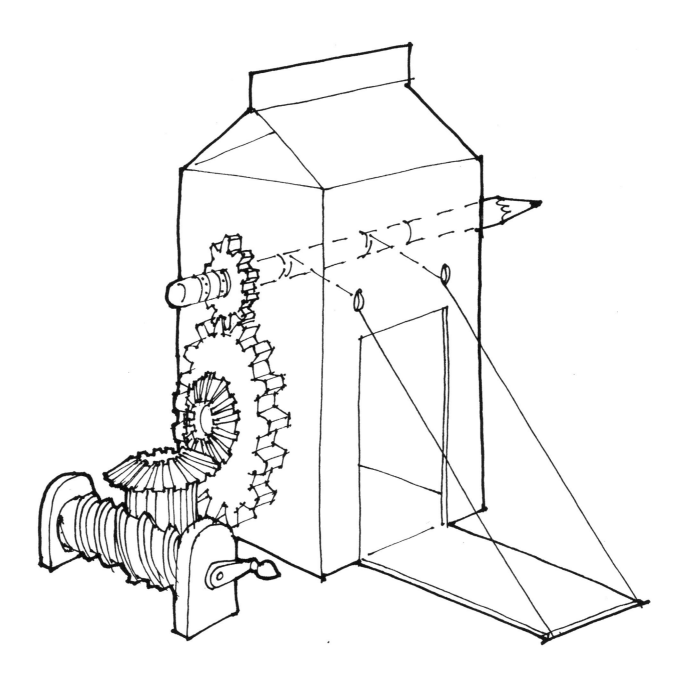

Designing and Building a Castle and Drawbridge

1. Draw a labelled diagram of your castle design.

2. Materials you will need:

_____ _____ _____

_____ _____ _____

_____ _____ _____

Portage & Main Press, 2008, Hands-on Science & Technology, Grade 4, BLM, ISBN: 978-1-55379-179-9

3. How will your drawbridge be raised and lowered?

_____

_____

4. What type of motion does your drawbridge use?

_____

5. Construct your castle. List any changes you made to your original design.

_____

_____

_____

6. Test your model.

7. Draw a labelled diagram of your completed castle.

Portage & Main Press, 2008, Hands-on Science & Technology, Grade 4, BLM, ISBN: 978-1-55379-179-9

9A

References for Teachers

Barton, Byron. *Machines at Work*. New York: Crowell, 1987.

Bilyk, Terry. *Let's Find Out!: Exploring Science in the World Around You*. Toronto: DC Heath Canada, 1993.

Bosak, Susan. *Science Is....* Richmond Hill, ON, Scholastic, 1991.

Cash, Terry. *101 Physics Tricks: Fun Experiments With Everyday Materials*. New York: Sterling Publishing, 1992.

Darby, Gene. *What Is a Simple Machine?* Chicago: Benefic Books, 1961.

Gray, Kathy Creaghan. *The Bridge From A–Z: Linking PEI and NB, Canada*. Cornwall, PEI: Quality Action Consulting, 1996.

Lafferty, Peter. *Forces and Motion*. Eyewitness Science Series. New York: Dorling Kindersley, 1992.

Metropolitan Toronto School Board. *101 Everyday Activities in Science and Technology*. Markham, ON: Pembroke Publishers, 1996.

Ollerenshaw, Chris, and Pat Triggs. *Wind-Ups*. Milwaukee: Gareth Stevens, 1994.

Potter, Tony. *Cars*. See How It Works Series. New York: Aladdin, 1989.

_____. *Earth Movers*. See How It Works Series. New York: Aladdin, 1989.

_____. *Planes*. See How It Works Series. New York: Aladdin, 1989.

_____. *Trucks*. See How It Works Series. New York: Aladdin, 1989.

Royston, Angela. *Planes*. Eye Openers Series. Toronto: Douglas & McIntyre, 1992.

_____. *Ships and Boats*. Eye Openers Series. Toronto: Douglas & McIntyre, 1992.

_____. *Trains*. Eye Openers Series. Toronto: Douglas & McIntyre, 1992.

_____. *Diggers and Dump Trucks*. Eye Openers Series. Toronto: Douglas & McIntyre, 1991.

_____. *Trucks*. Eye Openers Series. Toronto: Collier Macmillan, 1991.

Williams, John. *Toys and Games*. Austin, TX: Raintree Steck-Vaughn, 1998.

Understanding Matter and Energy

Unit 3: Light and Sound

Books for Children

Banyai, Istvan. *Zoom*. New York: Viking, 1995.

_____. *Re-Zoom*. New York: Viking, 1995.

Branley, Franklyn. *Day Light, Night Light: Where Light Comes From*. Let's Read and Find Out Science, Stage 2. New York: HarperCollins, 1998.

Brown, Marcia. *Walk With Your Eyes*. New York: Watts, 1979.

Brown, Margaret Wise. *The Country Noisy Book*. New York: HarperCollins, 1994.

Carle, Eric. *Hello, Red Fox*. New York: Simon & Schuster, 1998.

Cleaver, Elizabeth. *The Enchanted Caribou.* New York: Atheneum, 1985.

Cole, Joanna. *The Magic Schoolbus and the Electric Field Trip*. New York: Scholastic, 1997.

Dwyer, Mindy. *Aurora: A Tale of the Northern Lights*. Anchorage: Alaska Northwest Books, 1997.

Eyvindson, Peter. *The Missing Sun*. Winnipeg, MB: Pemmican, 1993.

Haas, Dorothy. *The Secret Life of Dilly McBean*. New York: Bradbury, 1986.

Joyce, William. *George Shrinks*. New York: Harper & Row, 1985.

Kincaid, Lucy. *The Ugly Duckling*. Windermere, FL: Rourke, 1983.

Lionni, Leo. *Geraldine, The Music Mouse*. New York: Pantheon, 1979.

Livingston, Myra. *Light and Shadow*. New York: Holiday House, 1992.

Locker, Thomas. *Anna and the Bagpiper.* New York: Philomel, 1994.

McDermott, Gerald. *Raven: A Trickster Tale from the Pacific Northwest.* New York: Harcourt, Brace, Jovanovich, 1993.

McGovern, Ann. *Too Much Noise*. Boston: Houghton Mifflin, 1967.

Meyrick, Kathryn. *The Lost Music: Gustav Mole's War on Noise*. New York: Child's Play, 1991.

Murphy, Jill. *Peace at Last*. New York: Dial Press, 1980.

Ryder, Joanne. *The Bear On the Moon*. New York: Morrow Junior Books, 1991.

Sandford, John. *The Gravity Company*. Nashville: Abingdon, 1988.

Silverstein, Shel. *Light in the Attic*. New York: Harper & Row, 1974.

_____. *Where the Sidewalk Ends*. New York: Harper & Row, 1974.

Simon, Seymour. *Einstein Anderson Shocks His Friends*. New York: Viking, 1980.

Stevenson, Robert Louis. *My Shadow*. New York: Putnam, 1990.

Waboose, Jan Bourdeau. *Morning On the Lake*. Toronto: Kid's Can Press, 1998.

Websites

- <http://www.opticalres.com/optics_for_kids/kidoptx_p1.html>

  The Optical Research Association's website includes information on light, prisms, lasers, and other topics, with explanations, diagrams, and links to further information.

- <http://www.exploratorium.edu/observatory/index.html>

  Exploratorium: Museum of Science, Art, and Human Perception in San Francisco. Visit the online observatory to view photographs of auroras and find answers to the most commonly asked questions regarding them.

- <http://www.emints.org/ethemes/resources/S00001566.shtml>

  Shadows: This site on shadows includes teacher's tips, links to information on opaque objects and telling time in ancient Rome, as well as activities for students to measure shadows and build their own sundials.

- <http://ww2010.atmos.uiuc.edu/(Gh)/guides/mtr/opt/home.rxml>

  Light and Optics: University of Illinois presents an online guide to atmospheric optics, such as rainbows, halos, and sunsets. Includes clear, concise answers as to why we see the colours that we do.

- <http://www.fi.edu/color/color.html>

  Light and Color: How do we see? Clear, simple explanations of light waves, wave travel, light transfer (reflected, absorbed, transmitted), and so on.

- <http://www.sciencetech.technomuses.ca/english/schoolzone/Info_Sound.cfm>

  Canada Science and Technology Museum's School Zone: Excellent resource for researching sound. Includes information on how sound is produced and carried, the speed of sound, frequency, sound waves, and how telephones work. The site includes links to games and the museum's Sound Connexion site.

- <http://library.thinkquest.org/11924/>

  Think Quest's "The Wizard's Lab": This site gives background information on sound and waves. Includes the answer to "what is sound?," properties of sound, characteristics of waves, and applications of waves (ultrasound, speakers).

- <http://www.sciencenewsforkids.org/articles/20070425/refs.asp>

  Cacophony Acoustics: This site includes links to articles on speaking to dolphins, noise pollution, and other topics, as well as games, puzzles, and teachers' resources.

- <http://www.fi.edu/fellows/fellow2/apr99/soundindex.html>

  Franklin Institute of Science: Educational site all about sound: the science of sound, how we hear, music, uses for sound, and further information.

- <http://www.civilization.ca/aborig/stones/instru/inmenu.htm>

  Musical instruments and noisemakers of First Nations Peoples of Canada: includes bullroarers, drums, calls, and rattles—locate each, by tribe or instrument.

▶

- **<http://micro.magnet.fsu.edu/optics/lightandcolor/vision.html>**

  Science, Optics, & You: An excellent resource for colour, including informative articles on colour perception, colour vision in humans, as well as near- and far-sightedness. The site includes activities and tutorials on topics such as the scientists associated with colour and light.

- **<http://yesmag.bc.ca>**

  Yes Mag is an online Canadian science magazine for children. Click on "How Does That Work?" to find information on the telescope, microscope, and binoculars—includes a short history, how the object works and its uses, diagrams, facts, and references.

- **<http://www.energyquest.ca.gov/index.html>**

  Energy Quest: Energy education from the California Energy Commission. Includes, with varying degrees of difficulty, energy science projects and puzzles and games. This site also contains biographies of scientists (Edison and Volto, for example), and tips for energy conservation.

- **<http://w3.rz-berlin.mpg.de/cmp/classmus.html>**

  The Classical Music Pages: This website provides extensive information concerning classical music—its history, biographical information about composers, and a dictionary of musical terminology. Click on "Composer's Name" to find an alphabetized listing of musicians: includes numerous sound bites.

- **<http://asa.aip.org/>**

  Acoustical Society of America: Click on "Listen to Sounds." Audio files of whale cries, trumpets and whistles, human-made underwater sounds, instruments, and musical scales. (Once your browser has downloaded the audio files, the sounds can be replayed quickly.)

- **<http://www.dsokids.com/>**

  Dallas Symphony Orchestra: Features string, wind, and percussion instruments (with sound bites), seating charts, information on composers, and a virtual tour.

Introduction

In this unit, students will also examine the unique characteristics of light and sound energy. Through hands-on investigations, students will learn how light travels, and will use this knowledge to construct simple optical devices. Similarly, students will learn how sound is created by vibrations, how it travels, and how a variety of sounds can be produced and controlled.

Students will also examine a wide variety of materials that transmit, reflect, and absorb light and sound energy. By investigating ways that these materials affect or are affected by sound and light, students will expand their knowledge of the properties of materials. They will also have opportunities to discover how the different properties of materials can help in designing products.

Science Vocabulary

Continue to use your science and technology word wall to display new vocabulary as it is introduced. Throughout this unit, teachers should use, and encourage students to use, vocabulary such as: *material, transparent, translucent, opaque, transmit, reflect, absorb, primary, sound waves, shadow, refraction, convex, concave, prism, spectrum, technology, scientist, optical device, vibration, pitch, frequency, inner ear, middle ear, outer ear, ear drum, cochlea, ear canal, ear bone, pinna, stringed instrument, wind instrument, percussion instrument, amplify,* and *volume.*

Materials Required for the Unit

Classroom: art paper, Bristol board, chart paper, clear tape, elastic bands, globe, index cards, magnifying glasses, markers, coloured pencils, masking tape, mural paper, overhead transparency markers, paint (red, yellow, blue), paintbrushes, paper (black, white), poster board, rulers, scissors, stapler, string, tagboard, thumbtacks, transparency film (clear and various colours), white glue

Books, Pictures, and Illustrations: *Walk With Your Eyes* (a book by Marcia Brown) or *The Ugly Duckling* (a book by Lucy Kincaid), pictures of rainbows, reference material on light technology, books about Thomas Edison, reference material on devices that amplify sound, *Why Didn't I Think of That?* (a book by Webb Garrison), *Too Much Noise* (a book by Ann McGovern)

Household: milk, spoons, towels, clear plastic wrap, drinking straws

Equipment: overhead projector, tape recorder or CD player, optical devices (e.g., glasses, telescopes, periscopes, kaleidoscope), piano, xylophone, variety of musical instruments (string, wind, and percussion), devices that amplify sound (e.g., megaphone, microphone), tape recorder

Other: transparent objects (e.g., eyeglass lens, overhead transparency sheets, water, clear glass, plastic wrap), opaque objects (e.g., cloth handerchiefs, paper, wood, coin, denim, aluminum foil, Styrofoam tray, plastic dish), translucent objects (e.g., wax paper, mesh, nylon stockings, stained glass, coloured cellophane, mist bottles, mirrors, tissue), flashlights, water, clay, dull and shiny metal, plastic (clear, frosted, coloured, solid), tissue paper, paper towel, construction paper, plastic bags (clear and coloured), wood, fabric samples: burlap, nylon stockings, and a variety of thick and thin weaves; large cardboard box that can be completely sealed, objects to place in cardboard box (e.g., black socks, plastic ball, book), items made of reflective materials (e.g., mirrors, bike reflectors, patrol vests), toothpicks, several objects that produce light (e.g., candles, oil lamps, electric lamps), jugs of water, glass jar, short section of garden hose, 3 pieces cardboard, clear glasses, various liquids (e.g.,

▶

corn syrup, oil, coloured water), large Ziploc bags, convex lenses, concave lenses, prisms, materials for constructing optical devices, rice, glass jars, metal tray, drum sticks, shallow pan of water, tuning forks, mallets, boards (20–30 cm long), small pieces of wood, fishing line, copper tubing, cardboard box lids, cardboard boxes, wooden dowels, materials for constructing musical instruments, recording of *The Country Noisy Book* (a story by Margaret Wise Brown), dog whistle, washers, toy car, screws, screwdrivers, wood blocks, bottle with cork, corkscrews

A Note About Materials

The materials needed to complete some activities are extensive. Teachers should review the materials lists for the unit ahead of time and make a note of items that students may be able to bring from home (for example, plastic containers, paper plates and/or cups, spoons, pie plates, fabric samples, balls of wool). Then, prior to beginning the lesson, teachers can send a letter home with students asking parents/guardians to donate some of these materials.

A Note About Safety

During their exploration of light and sound, students should be able to identify, and understand, the importance of some fundamental practices that will ensure their own safety and the safety of others. When studying the light portion of this unit, students need to know that looking directly at the sun can harm their eyes. They also need to know why sunlight reflected from a mirror should be aimed away from people's eyes and from materials that might be ignited. When studying the sound portion of the unit, students need to know why safe volume levels must be observed.

1 | Light Sources

Expectations

- **2.6** Use appropriate science and technology vocabulary, including *natural, artificial, beam of light, pitch, loudness*, and *vibration*, in oral and written communication

- **2.7** Use a variety of forms to communicate with different audiences and for a variety of purposes

- **3.1** Identify a variety of natural light sources and artificial light sources

- **3.2** Distinguish between objects that emit their own light and those that reflect light from other sources

- **3.7** Distinguish between sources of light that give off both light and heat and those that give off light but little or no heat

- **3.8** Identify devices that make use of the properties of light and sound

Science Background Information for Teachers

Light does not have weight and does not take up space. As a result, it is not matter. Light is one form of energy and, unlike sound, does not need a medium through which to travel. It can travel through a vacuum (sound cannot). *Luminous objects* are objects that give off their own light. *Illuminated objects* are objects on which light shines, enabling the observer to see them. Natural light sources include the sun, fireflies that flash or glow in the dark, and aurora borealis and aurora australis (dazzling displays of coloured lights that flicker in the sky in the northern and southern regions of the world). Artificial light is created by humans and includes oil lamps, electric lights, and candles.

Materials

- several objects that produce light, (e.g., flashlights, candles, oil lamp, lantern, electric lamp)
- magnifying glass (one for each group)
- jugs of water
- white paper, 4-cm square (one for each group)
- glass jars

Activity: Part One

Note: It is best to do this activity on a bright, sunny day in order to investigate sunlight. When investigating sunlight, stress to students that they are not to look directly at the sun, because, by doing so, they can permanently damage their eyes.

Take students outdoors, and have them investigate their shadows. Ask:

- Can you create a shadow of your body on the ground?
- How is the shadow created?
- What role does the sun play in creating a shadow?
- What other shadows can you see that are created when the sun shines on objects?
- Would you see shadows at night if there was no light? Why not?

Have students work in groups to further investigate sunlight. Give each group a 4-centimetre square piece of paper, a glass jar, and a magnifying glass. Have them place the paper in the glass jar.

Note: The paper in the glass jar may burn in this experiment. Have a jug of water on hand as a safety precaution. Remind students of the dangers of fire. Stress that this activity should never be done without adult supervision.

►

Have students hold the magnifying glass over the paper so that the light produces a bright spot on the paper. Have students adjust the distance of the magnifying glass so that a small, clear, bright spot is produced on the paper. Ask:

- What do you think is going to happen to the paper?
- Why do you think this will happen?

Have students carefully observe the bright spot on the paper. The paper will heat up, some smoke may be produced, and the spot will become brown.

After students have conducted this investigation, ask:

- What caused the bright spot on the paper?
- Where did the light come from?
- What caused the paper to turn brown?
- Where did the heat come from?

Activity: Part Two

Back in the classroom, display the various light sources. Allow students to examine and manipulate them. Ask:

- What is each item called?
- What do they have in common?
- How does each of them produce light?
- For each item, where does the energy come from to produce light?
- Do all of the items produce heat and light?

In groups, have students brainstorm a list of light sources and record these ideas on Activity Sheet A (3.1.1). Encourage students to include light sources found at school, in the home, and in the community. Also, have students describe how each object creates light (for example, a lamp uses electricity, a flashlight uses batteries).

After the groups have completed their activity sheets, have them share their ideas and discuss each light source. Ask:

- How is light created by the object?
- What source of energy is used?
- Is just light created, or is heat created as well?

Note: Be sure to discuss objects that reflect light, not just objects that create their own light. For example, the moon appears lit, because the sun's light reflects off it. The same is true of reflectors on bicycles, which reflect light from a car's headlights.

Activity Sheet A

Directions to students:

As a group, list several objects that produce light. Also, describe how light is produced by each object, and answer the question at the bottom of the paper (3.1.1).

Activity: Part Three

Have students begin a concept map to show their understanding of light. Throughout the unit, they can add to their concept maps.

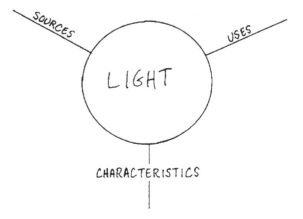

1

Activity Centre

On index cards, list several sources of light,
such as fireflies, fluorescent bulbs, neon lights,
lightning, lasers, and aurora borealis. Encourage
students to use reference books, encyclopedias,
and the Internet to research each of these
sources. Their research and diagrams can be
presented on large sheets of art paper that
can be put together to form a class book titled
Sources of Light.

Sources of Light

Light Source	How Light Is Produced

How is light helpful to humans and other living things?

_____

_____

_____

_____

Portage & Main Press, 2008, Hands-on Science & Technology, Grade 4, BLM, ISBN: 978-1-55379-179-9

2 | Light Travel

Expectations

- **2.2** Investigate the basic properties of light

- **2.6** Use appropriate science and technology vocabulary, including *natural, artificial, beam of light, pitch, loudness,* and *vibration,* in oral and written communication

- **2.7** Use a variety of forms to communicate with different audiences and for a variety of purposes

- **3.3** Describe properties of light, including the following: light travels in a straight path; light can be absorbed, reflected, and refracted

- **3.6** Describe how different objects and materials interact with light and sound energy

Science Background Information for Teachers

Light rays travel in a straight path. The rays bend, however, when they pass from one medium to another (for example, from air to water) because of their change in speed. Light travels more slowly through water than it does through air. The bending of light is called *refraction*.

Materials

- short section of garden hose
- flashlight
- 3 pieces of cardboard, 15 cm x 15 cm squares
- tape
- table or other flat surface
- jugs of water
- towels
- clear drinking glasses
- rulers
- scissors
- spoons
- various liquids such as corn syrup, oil, and coloured water

- pencils
- large Ziploc plastic bags

Activity: Part One

Display the garden hose in a coiled formation. Ask students:

- Do you think light can travel down the garden hose when the hose is coiled?
- What do you think will happen if you shine the flashlight down one end of the hose?
- Will you see the light at the other end of the hose?

Turn off the classroom lights, and test students' predictions by shining the flashlight down one end of the hose while it is still coiled. Ask:

- Can you see the light at the other end? Why not?
- What do you have to do to have the light travel through the hose?

Straighten the hose by having two students hold the ends so that the hose is taut. Shine the light through the hose, and have students observe if light is seen at the other end. Ask:

- What does this tell you about the way light travels? (It travels in a straight path.)

Now, set up the following apparatus:

Make a 3-centimetre square opening in the centre of each of the three pieces of cardboard. Place the cardboard pieces about 30 centimetres apart in a row, and tape them upright to a table. The square openings must be in a straight line so that the light from the flashlight shines through all three squares and onto the wall (see diagram on page 148).

Present the apparatus to students. Ask:

- What do you think will happen if I shine the flashlight through the first hole in the cardboard?

►

- How will the light travel?
- Where will you finally see the light?

Turn off the classroom lights, and test students' predictions by shining the flashlight through the holes in the cardboard. Ask:

- How does the light travel?
- Does light travel in a straight line?
- What do you think will happen if the second or third piece of cardboard is moved?

Test students' predictions by moving one piece of cardboard so the square openings are not in line. The light will not reach the wall.

Activity: Part Two

Have students work in groups. Have them fill a glass half full with water, place a pencil in the glass, and observe the pencil though the glass. Ask:

- What does the pencil look like?
- Is the pencil really bent at water level?
- Why do you think it looks as if the pencil is bent?

Introduce the term *refraction* to students. Explain that light bends as it passes through different materials (matter), making objects look different to the human eye.

Encourage students to move the pencil slowly around the inside of the glass and observe the pencil through the glass for any changes. They may be able to see the pencil change from one to two pencils, and even to half a pencil.

After students have investigated how the pencil looks in water, ask:

- Do you think other objects will look the same through the water?

Have students test objects, such as rulers and spoons, to see how each appears in the glass of water. They may also wish to experiment with other liquids, such as corn syrup, oil, and coloured water.

Note: The next investigation will further assist students in understanding refraction.

Provide each student with a sharp pencil, and have them rub the sharpened end with a towel so the lead is smooth. Have students fill a Ziploc bag with water and seal it. Now, have students push their pencils through both sides of the bags in one motion. (Keep towels on hand for leaks.) As students observe the pencil through the bag, they will again see how refraction causes the pencil to appear bent.

Activity Sheet A

Directions to students:

Draw and label diagrams that shows what the pencil and other objects looked like in the glass of water. Explain what you have learned about light in this investigation (3.2.1).

Extensions

- Have each student draw a large, thick arrow on an index card. Then, ask students to place the card about 10 centimetres behind a clear, empty glass. Have students look through the glass and note the direction the arrow is pointing. While students are watching the arrow, gradually pour water into the glass until the water level is above the index card. The arrow may appear a little fuzzy, but it should now be pointing in the opposite direction due to refraction.

- Have students investigate and research mirages, which occur because of refraction. A mirage appears when there is a clear sky and little wind. As the sun heats up the ground, the air closest to the ground becomes warmer than the air above. As the light passes from the warm air to the cool air, it bends (refraction). This causes you to see things that are not really there, like waves of water on the road, which are actually images of the sky on the road.

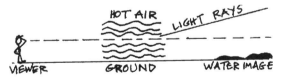

Assessment Suggestion

As students work in their groups, observe their abilities to conduct investigations and discuss the characteristics of light. Use the Anecdotal Record sheet, found on page 19, to record results.

How Light Travels

What did you learn about how light travels?

_____

_____

_____

_____

3 | Transparent, Translucent, and Opaque Materials

Expectations

- **2.2** Investigate the basic properties of light

- **2.5** Use scientific inquiry/research skills to investigate applications of the properties of light or sound

- **2.6** Use appropriate science and technology vocabulary, including *natural, artificial, beam of light, pitch, loudness,* and *vibration,* in oral and written communication

- **2.7** Use a variety of forms to communicate with different audiences and for a variety of purposes

- **3.3** Describe properties of light, including the following: light travels in a straight path; light can be absorbed, reflected, and refracted

Science Background Information for Teachers

Materials that block the light hitting them are called *opaque* materials. Materials that let light pass right through them are called *transparent* materials. Air, water, and clear glass are examples of transparent materials. Some materials are neither transparent nor opaque; they let just some light pass through them. These are called *translucent* materials. Frosted glass and wax paper are examples of translucent materials.

Materials

- transparent objects (e.g., eyeglass lens, overhead transparency sheets, water, clear glass, plastic wrap)
- opaque objects (e.g., cloth handkerchief, dark paper, wood, coin, denim material, aluminum foil, Styrofoam tray, plastic dish)
- translucent objects (e.g., wax paper, mesh, nylon stockings, stained glass, coloured cellophane tissue)
- overhead projector
- flashlight
- water
- milk
- black paper
- spoon
- mist bottle (clean, empty Windex spray bottle, for example)
- overhead transparency markers

Activity

Display the various opaque, translucent, and transparent objects. Allow students to examine and manipulate the objects. Discuss the objects' similarities and differences. Ask:

- How are the plastic wrap and the eyeglass lens the same?
- Which objects can you see through clearly?
- Which objects can you not see through at all?
- Which objects can you see through partially?

Invite students to shine a flashlight through several objects (for example, the eyeglass lens, cloth handkerchief, paper, wood, water, clear glass, coin, air, wax paper, and overhead transparency sheet). Have them observe how the light travels through each.

Provide each student with an overhead transparency sheet and marker. Have students print a secret message or draw a picture on their sheets. In turn, have students place their overhead sheets on the projector, select an object (such as a piece of cloth, glass, or wax paper), and place it over their message or picture. Turn on the projector, and have students observe how the light passes through the objects and whether or not the student's message can be seen.

▶

Note: Opaque objects will completely block the student's work. Translucent objects will distort the work or make it fuzzy. Transparent objects will allow the picture or message to be seen clearly.

Have students examine the various objects once again, to determine if each object's usefulness is related to its ability to transmit light. Ask questions such as:

- Why is it important that the lenses in eyeglasses be transparent?
- Why is it important that clothing be opaque?
- Why are hats opaque?
- Why are sunglass lenses translucent?

During this discussion, encourage students to use the terms *transparent, translucent,* and *opaque* when describing objects and materials.

Activity Sheet A

Directions to students:

List materials that are transparent, translucent, and opaque (3.3.1).

Extensions

- Divide a large table into three sections. Label the sections "Opaque," "Translucent," and "Transparent." Have students collect articles from the classroom and from home and place them in the appropriate sections on the table for display purposes.

- As a class, examine various liquids, such as oil, vinegar, water, milk, Kool-Aid, orange juice, and coffee. Have students classify the liquids as opaque, translucent, or transparent.

Assessment Suggestion

Have students complete a Student Self-Assessment sheet, found on page 26, to reflect on their own learning about transparent, translucent, and opaque objects.

Can You See Through Me?

A *transparent* object can be seen through clearly.

A *translucent* object can be seen through partly.

An *opaque* object cannot be seen through at all.

Transparent Object	Translucent Object	Opaque Object

3A

Portage & Main Press, 2008, Hands-on Science & Technology, Grade 4, BLM, ISBN: 978-1-55379-179-9

4 Light and Materials

Expectations

- **2.2** Investigate the basic properties of light

- **2.6** Use appropriate science and technology vocabulary, including *natural, artificial, beam of light, pitch, loudness*, and *vibration*, in oral and written communication

- **2.7** Use a variety of forms to communicate with different audiences and for a variety of purposes

- **3.3** Describe properties of light, including the following: light travels in a straight path; light can be absorbed, reflected, and refracted

Materials

- chart paper
- markers
- chart of transparent, translucent, and opaque materials made in lesson 1
- flashlights
- clay
- dull and shiny metal, including aluminum foil
- clear glass
- mirrors
- plastic: clear, frosted, coloured, and solid colour opaque
- paper: tissue paper, paper towel, construction paper
- plastic bags: clear and coloured
- wood
- cloths: nylon stocking, burlap, and a variety of thin and thick weaves

Activity

As a class, brainstorm a list of different types of light, including natural and human-made sources (for example, sunlight, flashlights, candles, neon lights, florescent lights). Record these ideas on chart paper.

Display the materials for the activity (clay, wood, metal, glass, mirrors, plastic, fabric, and so on) for students to examine. Review the terms *translucent, transparent,* and *opaque*. Ask:

- Which of these materials are transparent?
- Which materials are opaque?
- Which are translucent?

Have students classify the materials as transparent, translucent, or opaque, and discuss which materials are natural and which are human-made.

Title a sheet of chart paper "Predictions." Divide the chart paper into three columns, labelled "Materials That Transmit Light," "Materials That Reflect Light," and "Materials That Absorb Light."

Discuss the term *transmit*. Materials that transmit light allow the light to shine through them, either totally or partially (these include transparent and translucent materials). Demonstrate this concept by shining the flashlight on a piece of clear glass. Have students predict which of the materials displayed will transmit light. Record these predictions on the chart.

Introduce the term *reflect*. Materials that reflect light cause the light to bounce off the material and shine in a different direction (such as mirrors and shiny metals). Demonstrate this concept by shining the flashlight on a piece of aluminum foil. Have students predict which of the materials displayed will reflect light. Record these predictions on the chart.

Discuss the term *absorb*. Materials that absorb light do not allow light to pass through them and do not reflect the light. Instead, the light is absorbed into the material. Demonstrate this concept by shining the flashlight on various opaque objects, such as a dark sheet of paper, a hand, and a ruler. The light will illuminate the objects, but will not pass through them or be reflected by them. Have students predict which materials will absorb light. Record students' predictions on the chart.

Now, tell students they are going to test their predictions. Distribute a copy of Activity Sheet A (3.4.1) to each student. Divide the class into working groups. Provide each group with a flashlight and samples of materials to test. Have students complete their activity sheets.

Have the groups report their findings after they complete their activity sheets and compare these results to the predictions chart. After all the groups have reported their findings, ask:

- How are these materials used?
- Why is glass a good material to use for eyeglasses?
- Why would mirrors not be good for eyeglasses?
- Which materials produced shadows?
- Why are shadows created by these objects?
- Which materials are good for building houses? Why?

Continue to discuss the usefulness of objects based on the materials from which they are made (for example, sunglasses filter dangerous light rays, coloured medicine bottles limit light, car visors block sunlight from the eyes).

Activity Sheet A

Directions to students:

List each object or material tested, and use a checkmark to record whether it reflects, transmits, or absorbs light (3.4.1).

Extensions

- Locate three similar potted plants. Cover one plant with a clear plastic pop bottle, the second plant with a green plastic pop bottle, and the third plant with an opaque-painted plastic pop bottle. Have students observe the effects on the growth of these plants.

- Collect a large variety of translucent, transparent, and opaque objects. Have students identify the objects made of opaque materials. Place one opaque object on a table near a wall or projector screen. Have students predict the size, shape, and location of the shadow created by the object when a flashlight is shone on it. Repeat for each object. When discussing this activity, focus on the idea that opaque materials absorb light and thereby cast shadows.

Assessment Suggestions

- As students investigate materials that transmit, reflect, and absorb light, observe their ability to work as a group. Use the Cooperative Skills Teacher Assessment sheet, found on page 25, to record results.

- Have students complete a Cooperative Skills Self-Assessment sheet, found on page 27, to reflect on their ability to work together.

Light and Materials

Materials that *transmit* light allow light to shine through them, either totally or partially.

Materials that *reflect* light cause light to bounce off the material and shine in a different direction.

Materials that *absorb* light allow no light to pass through them and also do not reflect light.

Object/ Material	Transmits Light	Reflects Light	Absorbs Light

5 | Light Reflection

Expectations

- **2.2** Investigate the basic properties of light

- **2.5** Use scientific inquiry/research skills to investigate applications of the properties of light or sound

- **2.6** Use appropriate science and technology vocabulary, including *natural, artificial, beam of light, pitch, loudness*, and *vibration*, in oral and written communication

- **2.7** Use a variety of forms to communicate with different audiences and for a variety of purposes

- **3.3** Describe properties of light, including the following: light travels in a straight path; light can be absorbed, reflected, and refracted

- **3.6** Describe how different objects and materials interact with light and sound energy

Science Background Information for Teachers

Reflection occurs when a surface returns light that hits it. White material reflects light, whereas black material absorbs the light. That is why, to stay cooler during summer months, we wear light coloured clothing. Luminous objects—such as fire, light bulbs, stars, the sun, and even hot metals (molten metal gives off light)—make their own light. When you shine a light on a non-luminous object, you are able to see it, because it reflects light back to you.

Materials

- *Walk With Your Eyes*, a book by Marcia Brown or *The Ugly Duckling*, a book by Lucy Kincaid
- large box that can be sealed completely
- objects to be placed in the box (Include objects that have varying abilities to reflect light, such as black socks, aluminum foil,

plastic ball, book, and so on. For added excitement, consider having a class treat inside the box.)
- flashlight
- chart paper
- marker
- various items made of reflective materials, (e.g., mirrors, bicycle reflectors, patrol vests, Halloween costumes, reflective tape)

Activity

Note: Before starting the activity, make a mystery box. Take a large cardboard box, and cut a small peephole (about 5-cm square) in the top of it. Push a pencil through the side of the box to create a hole for a light source. Fill the box with an assortment of objects that have varying abilities to reflect light.

Read aloud the poems in *Walk With Your Eyes*. The book has many vivid pictures that you can share with students. There are some excellent examples of reflections in nature, including those that are on the front cover. An alternate opening to this activity is to read aloud the book *The Ugly Duckling*. The swan believes it is ugly until it finally sees its own reflection and realizes that it has become beautiful.

Following the reading, darken your classroom. Close curtains or cover windows. Turn off the lights, and display the mystery box for students to examine. Explain that there are a number of objects inside the box. Ask students:

- Can you discover a way of finding out what is inside the box without touching the box?

Have students look through the peephole. Ask:

- Can you see what is inside the box?
- Why is it difficult for you to see the objects?

Explain that objects cannot be seen when no light is available. Only objects that create their own light or that reflect light can be seen. Challenge students to think of ways they can see the objects. Turn the lights back on in the classroom. Ask students:

- Is there enough light now for you to see the objects inside the box?
- Why is it still difficult for you to see some objects?

Explain that some objects do not reflect light as well as others, so they are difficult to see when light is blocked. Have students shine the flashlight through the pencil hole on the side of the box and examine the objects inside. Ask:

- Can you name all the objects in the box now?
- Which ones can you see now that you could not see before?
- Why were these objects difficult for you to see?

Remove all the objects from the box, and have students examine them. Ask:

- Which objects were the easiest for you to see? Why?
- Which objects were the most difficult to see? Why?

Classify and arrange the objects according to how well they could reflect light (from most reflective to least reflective). On chart paper, make a list of materials that reflect light well.

Now, display all the reflective items for students to examine. Ask:

- Can you see these objects when the room is totally dark?
- Why or why not?

Turn off the lights in the classroom, and have students observe the objects. Ask:

- Can you see these objects in the dark?
- What do you need to see the objects better?

Have a student shine a flashlight toward the objects. Ask:

- Can you see all of the objects now?
- What happens to the objects when you shine the light on them?

Have students discuss how the light from the flashlight reflects brightly on objects such as reflectors and mirrors. Turn on the lights in the room, and further discuss the various objects. Ask:

- How are these objects important to you in your everyday lives?
- When do you need reflective objects?

Discuss the safety aspects of reflective material for cyclists, drivers, patrols, and pedestrians.

Activity Sheet A

Directions to students:

In the left-hand column, list objects and materials that reflect light well and in the right-hand column, list those that do not reflect light well. Write a paragraph to describe how reflective materials help you in everyday life, and include an illustrated example (3.5.1).

Extensions

- In a dark room, have students set a mirror on a table then shine a flashlight on the mirror. The reflected light should seem almost as bright as the flashlight beam. Try the same activity using a piece of aluminum foil instead of the mirror, and observe how the light is reflected. Finally, use a piece of crumpled foil (in a ball shape). The crinkles should cause the light to bounce in all directions.

Note: This activity shows that rough surfaces do not reflect light as evenly or as well as smooth surfaces do.

5

Repeat this activity using several small mirrors. Challenge students to set up mirrors in domino fashion to find out how many times they can reflect light. See if they can make the light travel right across the classroom.

- Have students shine a flashlight on a large piece of white paper. Have them hold their hands about 30 centimetre above the paper so their hands can pick up the light being reflected from the paper. Encourage them to observe how brightly lit their hands are from the reflected light. Now, repeat this with a large sheet of black paper. Since black absorbs light, not much light is reflected. Students' hands will not appear very brightly lit.

- Focus on how light and heat work together in reflection and absorption. Paint one juice can black and one can white. Fill both with water, place a thermometer in each can, and set the cans in direct sunlight. Observe and record the temperature of the water in each can. Since both heat and light are absorbed by the black coating on one of the cans, the water temperature inside the black can will be higher than the water temperature inside the white can. Light and heat are reflected off the white coating on the other can.

Relate this investigation to clothing selections for the seasons (for example, people usually wear lighter coloured clothing in summer than in winter to reflect heat and light).

- Investigate ways that finishing processes, such as paint, can alter an object's ability to transmit, absorb, or reflect light. Collect several reflective objects such as mirrors, coins, aluminum foil, jewellery, and glass ornaments. Place an object in a cardboard box, and shine a flashlight onto the object to see if light can be reflected off the object. After investigating the reflective qualities of several objects, paint some of the objects various colours, using washable powder paint. Once dried, test the objects again by placing them in the box and shining the flashlight on them. Have students observe and discuss how the paint affects the reflective ability of the objects.

Date: _____ **Name:** _____

Reflection

Objects That Reflect Light Well	Objects That Do Not Reflect Light Well

This is one way reflective materials help me in everyday life:

	_____

Portage & Main Press, 2008, Hands-on Science & Technology, Grade 4, BLM, ISBN: 978-1-55379-179-9

5A

6 | Colour Mixing

Expectations

- **2.2** Investigate the basic properties of light

- **2.5** Use scientific inquiry/research skills to investigate applications of the properties of light or sound

- **2.6** Use appropriate science and technology vocabulary, including *natural, artificial, beam of light, pitch, loudness*, and *vibration*, in oral and written communication

- **3.3** Describe properties of light, including the following: light travels in a straight path; light can be absorbed, reflected, and refracted

- **3.6** Describe how different objects and materials interact with light and sound energy

Science Background Information for Teachers

Visible white light from the sun is made up of the same colours that are in a rainbow (red, orange, yellow, green, blue, indigo, and violet). A rainbow, appears when water droplets in the air cause the sun's light rays to bend. The same colours can also been seen through a prism, which breaks white light into a *spectrum*.

Red, yellow, and blue are *primary colours*. This means that they can be mixed together to form *secondary* and *tertiary* colours.

Materials

- chart paper
- markers
- red, yellow, and blue paint
- paintbrushes
- art paper
- cardboard overhead transparency frames (These can also be made from Bristol board or tagboard cut into frames that will fit a sheet of transparency film.)
- coloured transparency film (various colours)

- clear transparency film (one sheet for each student)
- toothpicks
- white glue
- clear tape
- scissors
- flashlights

Activity: Part One

As a class, brainstorm a list of colours. Encourage students to identify as many colours as possible, including less common ones such as fuchsia, indigo, and persimmon. Record the colours on chart paper.

Divide the class into working groups, and provide each group with primary colour paints, paintbrushes, and art paper. Challenge the groups to use as many colours as possible to create artwork. Ask students:

- How can you use the three colours I gave you to create other colours?

Give students plenty of time to experiment with colour mixing to create their works of art.

Following the activity, distribute a copy of Activity Sheet A (3.6.1) to each student. Have students identify the colours they mixed together to create each colour on their pictures. Have them record their findings on their activity sheets.

Activity Sheet A

Directions to students:

Use the chart to record your ideas about colour mixing (3.6.1).

Activity: Part Two

Provide each student with a sheet of clear transparency film and a frame. Have students secure the film in the frame with clear tape.

Provide students with several sheets of coloured transparency film. Challenge them to create pictures by cutting out figures from the film and overlapping them to create as many new colours as possible. The figures can be combined and attached to the clear transparency film, using very small droplets of glue applied with toothpicks.

Note: Encourage students to use only small amounts of glue. When the glue dries, it may be visible.

Note: The colours created will look different to the naked eye compared to how they will look on an overhead projector. Encourage students to use a flashlight to transmit light onto their figures to see how the colour mixing will look on the projector.

When all students have created pictures, have them display the pictures for the class on the overhead projector. Discuss how various colours were combined or overlapped to create new colours.

Activity Centres

■ Provide students with cardboard, scissors, nails, paint, and/or markers. Challenge students to use colours and patterns of their own creation to make spinning colour wheels. Have students observe how the colours mix when the wheels spin.

Note: Also see the extension activities that use spinning colour wheels.

■ Have students create stained glass effects with coloured transparencies or cellophane. Also, have students try to make similar pictures with tissue paper and compare how light travels through each material.

Extensions

■ Have students make spinning colour wheels. From cardboard, cut out three circles, approximately 8 centimetres in diameter each. Divide the circles into three equal pie-shaped sections, and use paint or markers to colour the sections yellow, red, and blue. Punch a nail through the circles to create a spinning top. Observe the colours that are seen when the circle is spinning.

■ Make the same spinning tops using the colours of the spectrum (red, orange, yellow, green, blue, indigo, and violet).

■ Teachers can attach the colour wheel to a bit on an electric drill to create a faster and more even spinning action.

Note: The spinning wheel does not really mix the colours. The top spins so fast that our eyes/brain combine the different colours together into single colours of light.

■ While discussing how the eyes and brain are "deceived" by the colour wheel, introduce other optical illusions and three-dimensional pictures.

■ Read aloud *Hello, Red Fox,* a book by Eric Carle, to investigate complementary colours.

Date: _____   Name: _____

Colour Mixing

The three primary colours are:

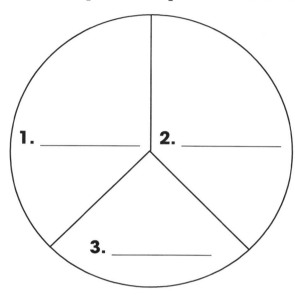

1. _____   2. _____

3. _____

Complete the colour-mixing chart:

[ ]	mixed with	[ ]	make → [ ]
[ ]	mixed with	[ ]	make → [ ]
[ ]	mixed with	[ ]	make → [ ]
[ ]	mixed with	[ ]	make → [ ]
[ ]	mixed with	[ ]	make → [ ]
[ ]	mixed with	[ ]	make → [ ]

My favourite colour that I created is _____ .

I made it by mixing _____ .

Portage & Main Press, 2008, Hands-on Science & Technology, Grade 4, BLM, ISBN: 978-1-55379-179-9

7 The Colours of Light

Expectations

- **2.2** Investigate the basic properties of light

- **2.6** Use appropriate science and technology vocabulary, including *natural, artificial, beam of light, pitch, loudness,* and *vibration*, in oral and written communication

- **2.7** Use a variety of forms to communicate with different audiences and for a variety of purposes

- **3.2** Distinguish between objects that emit their own light and those that reflect light from other sources

- **3.3** Describe properties of light, including the following: light travels in a straight path; light can be absorbed, reflected, and refracted

- **3.6** Describe how different objects and materials interact with light and sound energy

Science Background Information for Teachers

When you see a rainbow, you actually see seven bands of colour. They are, from outside to inside, red, orange, yellow, green, blue, indigo, and violet. The order is always the same, however, some bands may be wider than others. Rainbows are created by *refraction*. When conditions are right, water droplets in the air can act to separate the colours in sunlight (that is, the water droplets act as prisms, refracting and reflecting the sunlight and separating the colours), hence, creating the colours of the rainbow. Sometimes, you can see rainbows in fine sprays of water, such as from lawn sprinklers. The water droplets of the sprinkler act in the same manner as raindrops do, refracting, reflecting, and dispersing light.

Objects appear to be different colours because they reflect some of the colours in light and absorb other colours. If a chalkboard appears black, it is because the board absorbs almost all the light and all the colours. It hardly reflects back any light. A red stop light appears red, because it reflects only red light and absorbs all other colours. Snow appears to be white, because it reflects all colours equally.

Materials

- various pictures and books depicting rainbows
- clear glasses of water
- flashlights
- white paper
- convex lenses
- concave lenses
- prisms

Activity

As a class, discuss rainbows. Display the pictures of rainbows for students to examine. Ask:

- When have you seen a rainbow?
- What colours do you see in a rainbow?
- Are the colours always the same?
- Are they always in the same order?
- How do you think a rainbow is created?

Have students work in groups. Distribute a copy of Activity Sheet A (3.7.1) to each group. Give each group a glass filled with water, a flashlight, and a piece of white paper. Have one student shine the flashlight on the glass of water, making sure the light beam is shining through the middle of the water. Have another student hold a piece of white paper beside the flashlight, adjusting the paper position until a rainbow appears. Ask:

- What did you observe?
- Why do you think a rainbow was created when you shone the flashlight through the glass of water? (The glass of water acts like one large drop of water. The "water droplet"

bends (or refracts) the light and spreads out the colours. The colours separate because different wavelengths of light have different angles of refraction. The rainbow that appears in front of the glass, spreading back toward the light source, is light that has been refracted and reflected. Another rainbow can be found behind the glass, made up of light that was refracted but not reflected.)

Now, give students convex and concave lenses, prisms, and copies of Activity Sheet A (3.7.1). Allow them plenty of time to investigate the colours of light. Have the groups shine the flashlights at the convex lenses, concave lenses, and the prisms, and observe the results. On their activity sheets, have them record how the light reacted.

Note: The following diagram depicts how light reacts through a prism:

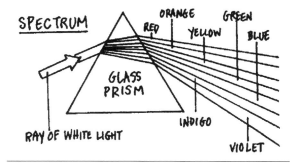

Activity Sheet A

Directions to students:

In the left-hand column, draw diagrams of how you shone light through the lenses and prism. In the right-hand column, record your observations of how light reacted when you shone the flashlight through the lenses and prism. Also, draw a diagram of a rainbow, showing the colours in the order that they are always seen (3.7.1).

Extension

On a bright, sunny day, take students outdoors. Bring along a piece of white paper and a clear glass, half full of water. Place the glass on the sheet of paper, and tip the glass back and forth. You will see spots of colours form on the paper. Try to produce all the colours of the rainbow. Ask students:

■ In what order are the colours?

■ Are some colours larger than others? (Each colour, or wavelength, is bent, or refracted, a different amount: the shorter wavelengths (those toward the violet end of the spectrum) are bent the most, and the longer wavelengths (those toward the red end of the spectrum) are bent the least.

For a variation of this activity, set a pan of water in direct sunlight. Place a mirror in the pan so that most of the mirror is underwater. Tilt the mirror so that reflected sunlight falls on a white surface, such as a sheet of paper. The colours of light will appear on the paper.

Note: Remind students to never look directly at the sun or at its reflection in a mirror.

Assessment Suggestions

■ As students conduct investigations in their groups, observe their abilities to work together. Use the Cooperative Skills Teacher Assessment sheet, found on page 25, to record results.

■ Have students complete a Cooperative Skills Self-Assessment sheet, found on page 27, to reflect on their own work in a group.

Colours of Light

Shining Light Through Objects	Observations
Convex Lens	
Concave Lens	
Prism	

Diagram of a rainbow:

Portage & Main Press, 2008, Hands-on Science & Technology, Grade 4, BLM, ISBN: 978-1-55379-179-9

8 | The Evolution of Light Technology

Expectations

- **1.2** Assess the impacts on society and the environment of light and/or sound energy produced by different technologies, taking different perspectives into account

- **2.5** Use scientific inquiry/research skills to investigate applications of the properties of light or sound

- **2.6** Use appropriate science and technology vocabulary, including *natural, artificial, beam of light, pitch, loudness*, and *vibration*, in oral and written communication

- **2.7** Use a variety of forms to communicate with different audiences and for a variety of purposes

Scientific Background Information for Teachers

Humans had been experimenting with light bulbs for 70 years before Thomas Edison invented the first practical light bulb. Edison was also the first scientist to design and construct a complete electrical distribution system.

Materials

- reference materials (nonfiction books, encyclopedias, the Internet)
- book or excerpt about Thomas Edison
- chart paper
- markers

Activity

Introduce light technology by discussing the importance of light in everyday life. Ask:

- How is light important to you?
- With what does the sun provide you?
- How do you use other forms of light?
- What would life be like if you had no source of light?

As a class, read books or excerpts about Thomas Edison. Ask:

- How did this scientist help humans?
- Why were his accomplishments important?

Challenge students to research other scientists involved and advances made in light technology. In groups, have students select a topic, then research, and, finally, present their findings to the class. Students can use Activity Sheet A (3.8.1) for compiling research, but they should be encouraged to display their research in an interesting way, such as with posters, plays, videos, or puppet shows.

As a class, identify criteria for students' research projects on light technology. Record these criteria on chart paper so that students can refer to them while conducting their research. Criteria should include:

- how the light energy produced by this technology impacts society
- complete diagram of the technology
- description of the technology
- information about the scientists involved in developing the technology
- project presentation
- oral presentation

Topics for research may include (but are not limited to):

- periscopes
- fibre optics
- telescopes
- cameras
- movie projectors
- lasers
- CD players
- holograms
- flashlights
- microscopes
- motion detectors

▶

- fluorescent lighting
- neon lighting
- halogen lighting

Activity Sheet A

Directions to students:

Use the activity sheet to organize your research on light technology (3.8.1).

Extension

Have each student create a page for a class big book titled *Light Technology*. Students can use the information gathered through research to present an illustrated informational page for the book.

Assessment Suggestion

Record the criteria developed by students on the Rubric sheet, found on page 23. As students present their projects, record results.

Light Technology Research

Topic: _____

_____

Diagram:

```

```

Description: _____

_____

_____

_____

Scientists: _____

_____

_____

_____

Portage & Main Press, 2008, Hands-on Science & Technology, Grade 4, BLM, ISBN: 978-1-55379-179-9

9 Designing and Constructing Optical Devices

Expectations

- **2.2** Investigate the basic properties of light

- **2.4** Use technological problem-solving skills to design, build, and test a device that makes use of the properties of light or sound

- **2.5** Use scientific inquiry/research skills to investigate applications of the properties of light or sound

- **2.6** Use appropriate science and technology vocabulary, including *natural, artificial, beam of light, pitch, loudness,* and *vibration,* in oral and written communication

- **2.7** Use a variety of forms to communicate with different audiences and for a variety of purposes

- **3.8** Identify devices that make use of the properties of light and sound

Science Background Information for Teachers

Kaleidoscopes have been popular toys for years. When you look through the viewing eyehole at one end of a kaleidoscope and rotate the tube, you see a changing variety of coloured patterns. The designs are produced with mirrors, which reflect images of bits of coloured glass.

A *periscope* is an optical device that allows you to see around corners and over walls and other surfaces. Periscopes are used in submarines to view above the surface of the water while the submarine is still submerged.

Materials

- various optical devices (e.g., glasses, magnifying lenses, telescope, periscope, kaleidoscope)
- materials for constructing optical devices (to be determined by students and collected by you and students)

Activity

Display the various optical devices for students to examine and manipulate. Review the research projects conducted previously. Ask:

- What are each of these optical devices called?
- How are they used?
- How do they help humans?

Challenge students to design and construct their own optical devices. Distribute a copy of Activity Sheet A (3.9.1) to each student. On the activity sheet, have them draw a diagram or blueprint of their design and list the materials required to construct it. Allow students plenty of class time to design their optical devices, collect materials, construct and test the devices.

Students can use suggestions from reference material, ideas acquired from the previous research project, as well as their own ideas. Suggestions for construction may include the following:

Kaleidoscope

Materials

- 3 pieces of card stock paper with silver Mylar on the back (2.5 cm x 10 cm)
- clear tape
- 5 clear, coloured, plastic beads
- toilet paper tube
- 2 pieces of paper towel
- 25–30 mL clear, plastic portion cup with lid

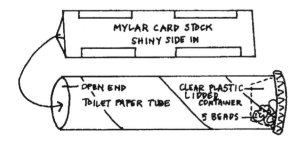

Instructions

1. Tape the three pieces of Mylar card stock together, with the mirrored sides facing inward, to form a triangular prism. (See top figure on page 170.)
2. Place five coloured beads in the plastic portion cup, and seal the cup with the lid.
3. Place the cup in one end of the paper tube roll. (See bottom figure on page 170.)
4. Wrap a paper towel around the triangular prism, and insert the prism into the toilet paper tube.

Use felt markers, coloured pencils, or paints to decorate the outside tube.

Point the plastic portion cup side toward a bright light source. Look through the open end of the tube, and slowly rotate the tube.

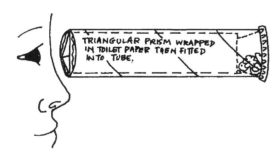

Periscope

Materials

- tape
- scissors
- 2 clean 1-litre milk cartons
- 2 small mirrors (8–9 cm square)
- paper towel

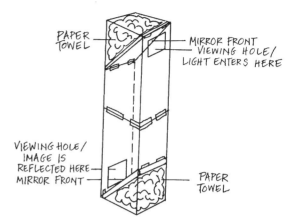

Instructions

1. Cut off the tops of the milk cartons.
2. Cut a 5-cm square viewing hole about 1.5 cm up from the bottom of each container.
3. Ball up a paper towel, and stuff it into the bottom corner of each of the containers, opposite the viewing hole.
4. Wedge the mirrors, reflective side facing up, on top of the paper towels. Push the bottom edge of the mirror down toward the side of the container with the viewing hole.
5. Ensure the angle of the mirror is about 45°. Tape the edges of the mirror to the carton.
6. Place the two cartons together, making sure that the viewing holes are on opposite sides. Tape the seams together.

Note: Remind students of the dangers of looking directly at light sources. Since the periscope contains mirrors, it can reflect harmful rays from the sun toward their eyes.

Magnifying Glass

Materials

- clear round container with tight-fitting lid (jar or pill bottle)
- water
- objects to examine (e.g., coin, reading material, leaves)

9

Instructions

1. Fill the clear, round container with water. Secure the lid, being careful not to spill any water.
2. Hold the container sideways, and bring it up to your eyes.
3. Look through the container at printed text, or at an object such as a coin, leaf, or rock. You will find that everything is magnified.

Activity Sheet A

Directions to students:

Design an optical device. Include a labelled diagram and a list of materials you will need. After constructing your optical device, test it, and evaluate your design (3.9.1).

Activity Centre

Have students place a small square of plastic wrap over some text (newspaper or book). Have them use an eyedropper to put single drops of water on the plastic, and observe the text underneath the droplets. Encourage students to make droplets of varying sizes, using different liquids to investigate magnification.

Note: The droplets act as a convex lens, magnifying the text.

Extension

Try different combinations of convex lenses, concave lenses, and mirrors in a paper tube to produce a simple optical device.

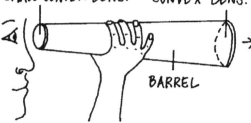

VIEWING END CAN BE HOLLOW, PLASTIC TRANSPARENCY, OR A SMALL CONVEX LENS.

OBJECTIVE END OF A REFRACTING TELESCOPE IS A CONVEX LENS.

BARREL

YOU COULD ALSO PUT ONE BARREL INTO ANOTHER TO SEE OBJECTS FARTHER IN THE DISTANCE.

Assessment Suggestion

Assess students' ability to design, construct, test, evaluate, and present their optical devices. Use the Individual Student Observations sheet, found on page 20, to record results.

Designing and Constructing Optical Devices

Optical device: _____

My design:

[   ]

Materials I need:

_____   _____   _____

_____   _____   _____

_____   _____   _____

How my device works: _____

_____

_____

Things about the design that I would change:

_____

_____

Portage & Main Press, 2008, Hands-on Science & Technology, Grade 4, BLM, ISBN: 978-1-55379-179-9

10 | Sound Vibrations

Expectations

- **2.3** Investigate the basic properties of sound

- **2.6** Use appropriate science and technology vocabulary, including *natural, artificial, beam of light, pitch, loudness*, and *vibration*, in oral and written communication

- **2.7** Use a variety of forms to communicate with different audiences and for a variety of purposes

- **3.4** Describe properties of sound, including the following: sound travels; sound can be absorbed or reflected and can be modified

- **3.5** Explain how vibrations cause sound

- **3.6** Describe how different objects and materials interact with light and sound energy

Science Background Information for Teachers

Sound occurs when tiny particles that make up air move back and forth quickly. Sound travels as waves of vibrating air. You hear sound when the sound waves reach your ear. Sound energy travels through air, water, and solid objects such as walls and buildings. When a tuning fork is vibrating, for example, tiny waves are produced. As the fork is placed in the water, the vibrations cause a small splash because the (sound) waves are travelling through the water. Sound needs matter through which to travel. In space, there is no air, so there is no sound.

Materials

- rice
- clear plastic wrap
- empty glass jars
- elastic bands
- metal tray
- drum sticks, spoons, or pencils
- shallow pan of water
- tuning forks

Activity: Part One

Divide the class into pairs of students, and give each pair an elastic band. Have one student stretch an elastic band between his or her index fingers while the other student plucks the elastic band. (You may wish to define and demonstrate the term *pluck*.) Have students observe the elastic band. Ask:

- What did you notice when the elastic band was plucked?
- What did you hear?
- What did you see?
- How was the sound created?

Focus on the sound created as the elastic band is plucked, and on the vibrating motion as the sound is heard. Introduce the term *vibration* as the "back and forth" motion of the elastic band. Ask:

- How do you think sound is created when you pluck the elastic band?

Explain that sound is created by vibrations that travel to the ear.

Activity: Part Two

Display several tuning forks, and give students an opportunity to examine and manipulate them. Ask:

- What is this object called?
- How does it work?

Have students take a tuning fork and tap the side of it. Ask:

- What do you observe when the tuning fork is tapped?
- Do you hear a sound?
- How is the sound produced?

10

Have students strike the tuning fork and then touch it. Ask:

- Do you feel something?
- What happens to the bars on the tuning fork when you strike it?
- What do you think will happen if you strike the tuning fork and then place it in water?

Have students test their predictions by striking the tuning fork and touching it against the still surface of water in a shallow pan. Ask:

- What happens to the water?
- Why do you think the water creates tiny waves or ripples?

Activity: Part Three

Divide the class into working groups. Distribute a glass jar, a piece of plastic wrap, an elastic band, and a few grains of rice to each group. Have the groups stretch a piece of plastic wrap tightly over the open end of a glass jar. Secure the plastic wrap with the elastic band. Place a few grains of rice on the plastic film. Ask:

- What do you think will happen if you hold the metal tray near the jar and bang the tray with a spoon or pencil?

Have students place the metal tray close to the jar and bang it with the spoon or pencil and observe what happens. (The sound waves from the tray cause the plastic wrap to vibrate and the grains of rice to move.)

Activity Sheet A

Directions to students:

Draw diagrams, and write explanations about your investigations with sound vibrations (3.10.1).

Extensions

- Have students gather around a turntable. Provide records for them to examine. Ask:

  - How do you think sound is made from a record?
  - What do you notice about the surface of a record?
  - Why do you think there are tiny grooves on the record?

  Place a record on the turntable, and have the students observe the needle as it moves on the groove. Ask:

  - Why is sound made when the needle moves on the grooves of the record?

  To further demonstrate how sound is created on a record, make a needle for the turntable by pushing a sewing needle through a cone-shaped paper cup. Turn on the turntable, and carefully place the point of the needle on a groove of the record. As the needle comes in contact with the grooves, the sound vibrations will travel up the needle and into the cone. The sound from the record will be clearly heard.

- Half fill a stemmed, thin-walled glass with water. Wash and dry your hands. Dip your index or middle finger in the water, and slowly run your fingertip around the rim of the glass. A humming sound will be produced. The sound is created when the friction from your finger movement causes the glass to vibrate. These vibrations can be seen in the water.

- Hold a ruler so that half of it extends over the edge of a tabletop. Bend the extended end down, and then quickly let it go. The vibrations of the ruler will create sound waves. The sound waves travel to your ear, enabling you to hear the sound.

10

■ Have students make kazoos. Have them place a piece of wax paper over the end of a short cardboard tube and secure the paper in place by wrapping an elastic band around the tube. Have students place their mouths loosely over the open end of the tube, without completely sealing the opening. Humming into the tube causes the wax paper to vibrate, creating a buzzing kazoo sound. This same effect is possible by covering a comb with tissue paper, placing your mouth against the comb, and humming.

Assessment Suggestion

As students conduct the various investigations, observe their abilities to demonstrate and explain the concept of sound vibrations. Use the Anecdotal Record sheet, found on page 19, to record results.

Sound Vibrations

Investigation 1: Elastic Band

Investigation 2: Tuning Fork

Investigation 3: Jar/Rice

Portage & Main Press, 2008, Hands-on Science & Technology, Grade 4, BLM, ISBN: 978-1-55379-179-9

11 | Pitch

Expectations

- **2.3** Investigate the basic properties of sound
- **2.5** Use scientific inquiry/research skills to investigate applications of the properties of light or sound
- **2.6** Use appropriate science and technology vocabulary, including *natural, artificial, beam of light, pitch, loudness*, and *vibration*, in oral and written communication
- **2.7** Use a variety of forms to communicate with different audiences and for a variety of purposes

Materials

- piano
- xylophone
- scissors
- glue
- mallets

Activity

Have students gather around a piano. Open the top of the piano, strike a key, and have students observe the hammer as it hits the wire string. Ask:

- Why is a sound made when you strike a piano key?
- What part of the piano vibrates?

Have students examine a long string in the piano. Ask:

- What kind of note do you think this string will make?

Have students observe as you strike the corresponding key. Ask:

- Was the note low or high?
- Why do you think this string made a low note?

Repeat this procedure with various strings and keys, discussing the relationship between the length of the string and the high or low sound of the note.

Use the term *pitch* to describe a high or low note. A long string on the piano creates a low-pitched note; a short string creates a high-pitched note. Ask:

- Why do you think long strings make low-pitched notes?
- Why do short strings make high-pitched notes?

Discuss the vibrations of the strings. Explain that a long string vibrates slowly, causing a low pitch. A short string vibrates very quickly, causing a high pitch. The speed at which the strings vibrate is referred to as *frequency*.

Discuss the thickness of the strings, noting that thick or heavy strings vibrate at a slower frequency, causing a lower pitch. Thin strings vibrate at a faster frequency, causing a higher pitch.

Have students examine an xylophone. Ask:

- What do you notice about the length and size of the bars on the xylophone?
- What kind of pitch do you think you will hear if you strike a short bar?
- What kind of pitch do you think you will hear if you strike a long bar?
- Why do the short bars make high-pitched notes?
- Why do the long bars make low-pitched notes?

Discuss again how pitch is related to the length and size of the bars, and how the frequency of the vibrations varies according to these variables.

11

Activity Sheet A

Direction to students:

In the picture, the bars of the xylophone have been taken off the instrument and mixed up. Cut out each bar, and order the bars from lowest pitch to highest pitch. Glue them to the xylophone in this order. Also, answer the questions (3.11.1).

Extension

Look at guitars and violins to see how different pitches are created. When your finger is placed on a string, the string is shortened, causing a higher pitch. The farther down on the neck of the instrument you place your finger, the higher the pitch will be.

High Pitch/Low Pitch

lowest pitch   highest pitch

Why does a long bar make a low pitch? _____

_____

Why does a short bar make a high pitch? _____

_____

What does the word *frequency* mean? _____

_____

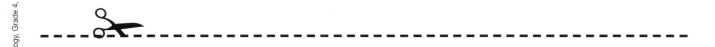

Portage & Main Press, 2008, Hands-on Science & Technology, Grade 4, BLM, ISBN: 978-1-55379-179-9

11A

12 | Musical Instruments

Expectations

- **2.3** Investigate the basic properties of sound

- **2.4** Use technological problem-solving skills to design, build, and test a device that makes use of the properties of light or sound

- **2.5** Use scientific inquiry/research skills to investigate applications of the properties of light or sound

- **2.6** Use appropriate science and technology vocabulary, including *natural, artificial, beam of light, pitch, loudness*, and *vibration*, in oral and written communication

- **2.7** Use a variety of forms to communicate with different audiences and for a variety of purposes

- **3.4** Describe properties of sound, including the following: sound travels; sound can be absorbed or reflected and can be modified

- **3.6** Describe how different objects and materials interact with light and sound energy

- **3.8** Identify devices that make use of the properties of light and sound

Science Background Information for Teachers

Note: This lesson introduces students to musical instruments and to the various ways in which sound is produced on them. Students are also given opportunities to construct models of simple string, percussion, and percussion instruments.

Musical instruments are classified by how the instrument produces its sound. The three major instrument groups are strings, wind, and percussion.

String instruments produce sound by a string being plucked or bowed. A guitar produces sound when the strings are plucked with fingers or with a pick. Violins and cellos produce sound when a bow is drawn over the strings. Pitch is changed by changing the length of the vibrating string. By pushing down on the string with a finger, the length is shortened, which produces a higher pitch sound. Thicker diameter strings also produce lower pitch.

Wind instruments produce sound when air is blown through the instrument. In brass instruments, such as the trumpet and trombone, the lips produce the vibration. Pitch is changed by using the valves or slides on the instrument. In the woodwind instruments, the reed in the mouthpiece produces the vibrations. In a flute or piccolo, the air itself vibrates in the column of the instrument to produce the sound. The length of the air column affects the pitch. A larger instrument like a saxophone will have a lower sound than a clarinet.

Percussion instruments produce sound by being struck. Bells, cymbals, and drums are percussion instruments. When you hit these instruments, they vibrate. The vibrations cause changes in air pressure. The air vibrates, and your ears hear these vibrations as sound. Most percussion instruments do not produce a pitch, so they are often called *rhythm instruments*. The piano and xylophone can produce a definite pitch, yet, they are still classified as percussion instruments, because the strings of the piano and bars of the xylophone are struck.

Materials

- chart paper
- thumbtacks
- boards (20–30 cm in length) (thickness and width are not important)
- small pieces of wood (about 1–2 cm in thickness, 1 cm in width x 5 cm in length)
- elastic bands (various thicknesses)
- fishing line
- copper tubing (5 or 6 tubes of various lengths)
- 8 drinking straws (milkshake size)
- clear tape
- scissors

12

- cardboard box lids
- cardboard boxes (Kleenex boxes are good)
- wooden dowels
- string
- mallet
- markers
- index cards
- masking tape
- variety of stringed, wind, and percussion instruments
- coloured pencils

Note: This is an excellent opportunity to request the support of your school music teacher or a music teacher from a local secondary school. You may also wish to invite a member of a local symphony or band to present to the class.

Activity: Part One

Display a variety of musical instruments for students to examine and manipulate. Have students identify as many instruments as they can by name. Record the names of these instruments on index cards, and display the cards on chart paper. As each instrument is identified, ask:

- How is sound made from this instrument?
- What does the musician have to do to make music?
- What kinds of sounds does the instrument make?

After all instruments have been discussed, demonstrate how each instrument makes music, and have students attempt to create sound from each. Ask:

- How was the sound created?
- Could you see or feel vibrations?
- Was the pitch of the instrument high or low?

Now, have students review all of the instruments named on the index cards. Challenge them to find ways to sort and classify the instruments.

Note: Students may devise several ways of grouping the instruments, such as by pitch, size, appearance, or according to how sound is made (wind, strings, percussion). These terms (*wind, string, percussion*) can be introduced to students, and students can be encouraged to use the terms as they study, design, and build musical instruments.

Activity Sheet A

Directions to students:

Classify the instruments by the way sound is made (percussion: something is struck; wind: air is blown through the instrument; and strings: the strings are plucked or strummed). Use one colour of coloured pencil to circle all instruments that belong in the same group. Make a legend for your page (3.12.1)

Activity: Part Two

Provide students with opportunities to make their own musical instruments. You may choose to build several instruments (wind, strings, percussion) as a prelude to the next activity, when students will be challenged to design and build their own unique instruments.

Provide students with boards, thumbtacks, small pieces of wood, and fishing line. Have students make one-stringed instrument (as in the diagram below). By pressing a finger against the string at different locations, different pitches can be created.

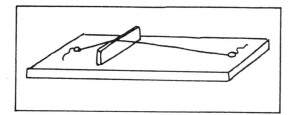

Students can use cardboard box lids, wooden dowels, and elastic bands to make simple harps. The fixed angle of the wooden dowels

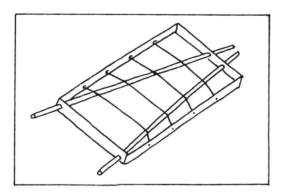

determines the length of each string, so various pitches are created when the strings are plucked (see diagram above).

Xylophones (below) can be constructed from string and copper piping cut to various lengths. The string is wound and taped around each piece of pipe, from shortest to longest in length. When the xylophone is held up and a pipe is struck with a mallet, a note sounds. The different lengths of piping will create various pitches.

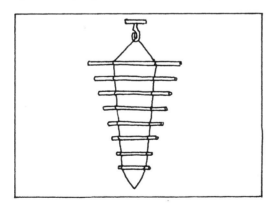

Have students discover how pitch is related to the thickness of strings. Provide small cardboards boxes with the top cuts off (Kleenex boxes are good for this activity). Also, provide several elastic bands of the same length but of different thicknesses. Have students stretch these elastic bands around the box so that the elastic extends over the top. When the bands are plucked, students will notice that the thick

bands create lower pitches, while the thin bands create higher pitches. (Thick bands vibrate more slowly than thin bands. This slower frequency creates a lower pitch.)

Have students experiment with sound as it relates to air and open columns. Have them cut straws to various lengths, flatten one end of each straw, and cut the flat end to point. By blowing through the other end of the straw, sound will be created. The short straws will create higher-pitched notes, because the frequency of the vibrations is faster. The longer straws will create low-pitched notes, because the frequency is slower. Challenge students to arrange the straws in order from lowest pitch to highest pitch. The straws can then be taped together to make a pan flute (see below).

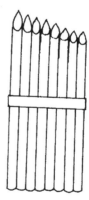

After students have built each instrument, have them experiment with the sounds they can create. Ask:

■ How is the sound made with this instrument?
■ How can you make a high-pitched sound?
■ How can you make a low-pitched sound?
■ How could you change or modify the instrument to create more sounds?

▶

12

Activity Sheet B

Directions to students:

Draw a diagram of one of the instruments you made. Label your diagram. Now, describe how sounds are made with the instrument (3.12.2).

Activity Centres

■ At an activity centre, provide six or seven glass drink bottles (300-mL size), a rubber mallet or drumstick, jugs of water, and a funnel. Have students pour different amounts of water into each glass, then gently strike each glass bottle with the mallet. The water vibrates, producing a sound. Students will notice that the bottles containing more water create lower-pitched notes, because the column of water is longer. Challenge students to create various notes and play simple tunes such as "Mary Had a Little Lamb" or "Do, Re, Me."

■ At an activity centre, provide empty pop bottles, jugs of water, and a funnel. Explain to students that by pouring different amounts of water into the bottles, the length of the open column of air is altered. If a lot of water is poured into a bottle, the open column becomes very short; therefore, when they blow into the bottle, the pitch is high. The resonating chamber (column of air) is short so the vibrations are fast, producing a high pitch. As the water level is lowered, the open column becomes longer and the pitch becomes lower. Students will find that this activity is the reverse of the preceeding one. When water is added in the preceeding activity the pitch goes down. When water is added in this activity, the pitch goes up.

Extensions

■ Make an instrument called *Household Bells*. Tie a string between two chairs so that the string is taut. Use short pieces of string to attach a hanger, a spoon, a fork, a ruler, and a pencil to the horizontal string so that it looks like a clothesline. Working with a partner or in small groups, have one student place his or her ear against the string. Have another student tap the different objects with the metal spoon. The student listening to the string should hear sound from the string and feel some vibrations. Have students try other objects like plastic forks, aluminum pie plates, and so on. Ask:

■ Which objects produce the best sound?
■ Which objects produce the most interesting sounds?

■ Have students make grass whistles. Ask them to choose a blade of grass 12–15 centimetres long. Have students hold the blade of grass between their thumbs with their hands closed in a praying position. The edge of the blade should face the student. Make sure the balls of students' hands are below their thumbs and the tops of both thumbs hold the grass firmly. Now, have students blow steadily through their thumbs. Have them practise until they get a smooth sound, adjusting the tension of their hands to produce different sounds. Have them try other varieties of grass to find out if they produce different sounds.

■ Make other musical instruments as a class or at a centre. For example:

Tambourine: two paper or pie plates secured together, with rice, beans, or buttons inside

Drums: milk cartons, cereal boxes, Kleenex boxes, and so on, with paper or fabric placed inside to dampen the sound

12

Rattles/maracas/drums: potato chip cans (with plastic lids) or margarine tubs filled with dried beans

Guitars: string different lengths of wire, fishing line, or elastic bands between nails on a board

Xylophone: soft drink bottles filled with water

Steel drums: assorted tin cans and metal bowls

Musical Instruments

Legend	Percussion	Wind	Strings

Portage & Main Press, 2008, Hands-on Science & Technology, Grade 4, BLM, ISBN: 978-1-55379-179-9

Making Musical Instruments

Instrument _____

How are the sounds made with this instrument?

_____

_____

_____

_____

_____

_____

_____

_____

_____

Portage & Main Press, 2008, Hands-on Science & Technology, Grade 4, BLM, ISBN: 978-1-55379-179-9

13 Designing Musical Instruments

Expectations

- **2.4** Use technological problem-solving skills to design, build, and test a device that makes use of the properties of light or sound

- **2.5** Use scientific inquiry/research skills to investigate applications of the properties of light or sound

- **2.6** Use appropriate science and technology vocabulary, including *natural, artificial, beam of light, pitch, loudness*, and *vibration*, in oral and written communication

- **2.7** Use a variety of forms to communicate with different audiences and for a variety of purposes

Note: In this lesson, students are given the opportunity to use what they have learned about musical instruments to design and construct their own instruments.

Materials

- variety of materials for making musical instruments (identified by students)
- chart paper
- markers

Activity

As a class, review the three families of musical instruments (wind, percussion, stringed), along with the instruments made in the previous lesson. Now, challenge students to design and build their own unique instruments.

Provide students with plenty of time to plan, design, and draw blueprints of their musical instruments. They should be encouraged to plan their projects first, create blueprints, and make modifications and improvements during the construction process. Students can use Activity Sheet A (3.13.1) to show the design and list the materials needed. As the students identify the materials they will need, collect these as a class.

Note: During construction of the instruments, stress the importance of safety procedures, such as using tools and materials safely. Loud noise is also a safety concern; students need to be careful not to produce volumes that may be harmful to others.

As a class, and before students present their instruments, identify four criteria that should be part of their presentations. This may include:

1. Description of how instrument creates sound
2. Explaination of how you can change the pitch
3. Explaination of how you can change the volume
4. What you would do differently if you could re-design the instrument

Record the criteria on chart paper, and have students respond to these criteria on their activity sheets. This will prepare them for their final presentations.

Activity Sheet A

Directions to students:

Draw a design for your instrument. Label your diagram. List the materials you will need to make your instrument. Now, plan your presentation by recording your ideas and responding to the class criteria (3.13.1).

Assessment Suggestions

- As students present their invented musical instruments, observe their ability to address the criteria identified by the class. List these criteria on the Rubric sheet, found on page 23, and record results during presentations.

- Have students complete a Student Self-Assessment sheet, found on page 26, to reflect on their own learning while designing and constructing a musical instrument.

Date: _____   Name: _____

Designing a Musical Instrument

Design of my musical instrument:

Materials I need:

_____   _____   _____

_____   _____   _____

_____   _____   _____

Class criteria for presentation:

1._____

2._____

3._____

4._____

5._____

Portage & Main Press, 2008, Hands-on Science & Technology, Grade 4, BLM, ISBN: 978-1-55379-179-9

14 Amplifying Sound

Expectations

- **2.3** Investigate the basic properties of sound

- **2.6** Use appropriate science and technology vocabulary, including *natural, artificial, beam of light, pitch, loudness*, and *vibration*, in oral and written communication

- **2.7** Use a variety of forms to communicate with different audiences and for a variety of purposes

- **3.4** Describe properties of sound, including the following: sound travels; sound can be absorbed or reflected and can be modified

Materials

- several devices that amplify sound (e.g., megaphones, microphones and speakers)
- tape-recorded story such as *The Country Noisy Book* by Margaret Wise Brown
- CD player or tape recorder
- reference material (e.g., Internet, encyclopedias) on devices that amplify sound
- poster board
- markers

Activity: Part One

Play a recorded story (such as *The Country Noisy Book*) for students to listen to. Stop the recording partway through, then have the class accompany you outside. Take the CD player or tape recorder with you. When you are outside, continue to play the recorded story at the same volume as it was in the classroom. Ask students:

- Can you hear the recording of the story as well outside as you could hear it in the classroom?
- Why not? (The sound waves bounce off the walls in a classroom, allowing us to hear sounds. Outdoors, the sound waves dissipate more, so sounds are more difficult to hear.)
- What could you do so you can hear the story better outside?

Increase the volume on the tape recorder or CD player, and continue to listen to the story. Discuss the sounds and events in the story.

Activity: Part Two

Back in the classroom, display devices that amplify sound. Have students examine and manipulate the devices. Discuss each item, and ask:

- What is this called?
- What is it used for?
- How do you think it works?

Have students demonstrate how they think each item works. Ask:

- When would you use a megaphone?
- Why do you need a megaphone outside, but not in the classroom? (Outside, the sound waves are not contained by the classroom walls.)
- When would you use a microphone and speaker?
- Why do you need a microphone in a large room, such as a gym or a theatre, but not in a smaller room, such as a classroom? (Sound waves dissipate more in a large room, and there is usually more noise from the audience, which competes with the sounds you want to hear.)

Divide the class into working groups, and have each group select, for research purposes, one device that amplifies sound. Have the groups use the reference material provided, as well as library resources, to gather information. Have students use Activity Sheet A (3.14.1) as a guide

14

for their research. Students can then use the information they have collected to help them create posters about devices that amplify sound.

Activity Sheet A

Directions to students:

Select a device that amplifies sound. Gather information about the device. Use the activity sheet as a guide for creating a research poster (3.14.1).

Activity Centre

Have students make the following toy, which involves sound amplification. Provide pieces of string (30–40 centimetres long), paper or Styrofoam cups, and nails. Have students poke a nail through the middle of the bottom of the cup, pull the string through the hole, and knot the end of the string that is inside the cup. The knot will prevent the string from being pulled out the bottom of the cup. Have students pull the other end of the string with their thumb and forefinger. They should hear a sound. Now, wet the string with water. The sound should become louder. The water produces more friction, and that increases the sound volume. The cup also helps to amplify the sound by acting as a cavity that allows the sound to bounce back and forth inside it. The back and forth movement of sound is called *resonance* and is found in instruments like the guitar and violin.

Extensions

■ Invite a guest who uses a hearing aid to demonstrate and explain to the students how the device works.

■ Go to a concert hall to hear a concert. Try to arrange a backstage tour. Encourage students to observe how the design of and materials used to build the hall ensure that everyone in the audience can hear well. (Many halls have cordless headphones for those with hearing conditions. This way the volume can be adjusted individually.)

Amplifying Sound

Create a poster about a device that amplifies sound. Make sure your poster includes the following:

1. Title: _____

2. Diagram:

3. How the device amplifies sound: _____

_____

_____

_____

_____

Portage & Main Press, 2008, Hands-on Science & Technology, Grade 4, BLM, ISBN: 978-1-55379-179-9

15 | Safety and Sound

Expectations

- **1.1** Assess the impacts on personal safety of devices that apply the properties of light and/or sound, and propose ways of using these devices to make our daily activities safer

- **2.5** Use scientific inquiry/research skills to investigate applications of the properties of light or sound

- **2.6** Use appropriate science and technology vocabulary, including *natural, artificial, beam of light, pitch, loudness*, and *vibration*, in oral and written communication

- **2.7** Use a variety of forms to communicate with different audiences and for a variety of purposes

Science Background Information for Teachers

Sound waves move sound energy from one place to another. A jet engine makes a great deal of sound energy. The engine sounds loud when the plane is close, yet, you can still hear the noise when the plane is several kilometres away.

The intensity of sound is measured in *decibels*. A purring cat measures 10 decibels; a jumbo jet engine measures around 120 decibels. Sounds over 130 decibels can seriously damage a person's hearing. Constant exposure to loud sounds can also damage hearing. Many rock musicians perform nightly in conditions of around 100 decibels. Hearing loss is of great concern for them.

Differences among sounds are due to differences in quality, loudness, and pitch.

Materials

- chart paper
- felt markers
- pencils
- *Too Much Noise*, a book by Ann McGovern

Activity: Part One

Divide the class into working groups, and provide each group with chart paper and markers. Challenge the groups to list as many reasons as they can why sound/hearing is important. Encourage them to think of a variety of issues, such as quality of life, safety, health, and the survival of other living things. Have the groups share their ideas with the class and add to the lists during discussion. Ideas may include:

- communicating with other people
- enjoying music and dance
- hearing sirens, fire alarms, horns honking
- doctor using a stethoscope to hear heart beats and breathing
- animals using sound to communicate with each other
- birdwatchers identifying birds by their songs

As you discuss the importance of sound and hearing, have students provide ideas on what it would be like to be deaf, and how they think deaf people communicate.

Activity: Part Two

Read aloud the story *Too Much Noise*. Discuss the sounds in the story, and have students determine which sounds are pleasant and which sounds are noise.

Divide the class into groups, and have students in each group discuss sounds that they like and dislike. Provide each group with Activity Sheet A (3.15.1) and pencils for recording their ideas. Encourage students to discuss why they like or dislike each sound.

Have the groups present their findings to the class, giving reasons for their likes and dislikes.

15

Discuss noise pollution as sounds that are generally not liked, and that may even be harmful to our ears. Ask students:

- Which sounds do you think could be harmful to your ears?
- What do you think loud noises do to your ears?
- Do your ears sometimes hurt, or do you get a headache from loud noises?
- How can humans protect their ears from loud noises?

Discuss ways that humans protect their ears, (for example, using earplugs and headphones on construction sites, at airports, and at other job locations where there are loud noises).

Discuss ways that humans try to cut down on noise (for example, placing restrictions on airplanes flying over cities, using snowblowers and lawn mowers only within specified hours, putting mufflers on cars and motorcycles).

Activity Sheet A

Directions to students:

List sounds that you like and dislike (3.15.1).

Extensions

- Create a concept map that shows sounds heard in various workplaces. For example:

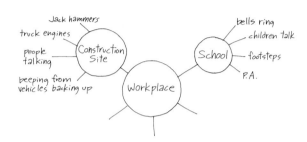

- Invite a guest speaker to the classroom to discuss the ways that deaf people communicate and use devices to help them in daily life. Encourage students to learn a few signs in American Sign Language (ASL).

- Invite a guest speaker from a local organization for the deaf or from the workplace safety department of a local heavy industry. Have your guest speak to students about hearing loss and injuries, and how they can protect their ears from harm.

- Have students design and construct headphone sets that stop external sounds. Have students compare their designs and test their effectiveness. Modify this activity by having students make covers for the speaker of a CD player or tape recorder. Have them experiment with different materials and thicknesses to find the best insulator for the sound.

Sound Likes and Dislikes

Sounds We Like	Sounds We Dislike

Portage & Main Press, 2008, Hands-on Science & Technology, Grade 4, BLM, ISBN: 978-1-55379-179-9

References for Teachers

Bosak, Susan. *Science Is....* Richmond Hill, ON: Scholastic, 1991.

Broekel, Ray. *Experiments With Light*. Chicago: Children's Press, 1986.

Brown, Robert. *200 Illustrated Science Experiments for Children*. Blue Ridge Summit, PA: Tab Books, 1987.

Dorling Kindersley Ultimate Visual Dictionary. New York: Dorling Kindersley, 1994.

Harlow, Rosie, and Gareth Morgan. *175 Amazing Nature Experiments*. New York: Random House, 1992.

Hirschfeld, Robert, and Nancy White. *The Kids' Science Book*. Milwaukee: Gareth Stevens, 1997.

Lamb, Herb, et al. *Science Today*. Austin, TX: Steck-Vaughn, 1987.

Markle, Sandra. *Discovering Science Secrets*. New York: Scholastic, 1991.

Murphy, Pat, Ellen Klages, and Linda Shore. *The Science Explorer*. Austin TX: Holt, 1996.

Rockcastle, Verne, et al. *Science*. Reading, MA: Addison-Wesley, 1984.

Rowe, Julian, and Molly Perham. *Using Energy*. Chicago: Children's Press, 1997.

Scott, Corinn Codye. *Chemistry*. Upper Saddle River, NJ: Querus, 1986.

Smolinsky, Jill, Carol Amato, and Eric Ladizinsky. *50 Nifty Super Science Fair Projects*. Chicago: RGA Publishing Group, 1996.

Suzuki, David. *Looking at the Environment*. New York: Wiley & Sons, 1992.

Varnado, Jewel. *Basic Science for Living*. Austin, TX: Steck-Vaughn, 1985.

White, Laurence B. *Science Games and Puzzles*. Chicago: Children's Press, 1997.

Willow, Diane, and Emily Curran. *Science Sensations*. Reading, MA: Addison-Wesley, 1989.

Understanding Earth and Space Systems

Unit 4: Rocks and Minerals

Books for Children

Arem, Joel E. *Rocks and Minerals: All Colour Guide*. Phoenix: Geoscience Press, 1991.

Baylor, Byrd. *Everybody Needs a Rock*. New York: Atheneum, 1974.

Blobaum, Cindy. *Geology Rocks!: 50 Hands-On Activities to Explore the Earth*. Charlotte, VT: Williamson, 1999.

Challoner, Jack. *Learn About Rocks and Minerals*. Learn About Series. Dayton, OH: Lorenz Books, 2008.

_____. *Rocks and Minerals*. Young Scientist Concepts & Projects. Milwaukee: Gareth Stevens, 1999.

Faulkner, Rebecca. *Igneous Rock*. Chicago: Raintree, 2007.

_____. *Metamorphic Rock*. Chicago: Raintree, 2007.

_____. *Sedimentary Rock*. Chicago: Raintree, 2007.

Gallant, Roy, A., and Christopher J. Schuberth. *Discovering Rocks and Minerals: A Nature Guide to Their Collection and Identification*. New York: Natural History Press, 1987.

Hewitt, Sally. *Rocks and Soil: Gems, Metals, and Minerals*. North Mankato, MN: Stargazer, 2008.

Oliver, Ray. *Rocks & Fossils*. London, UK: Hamlyn, 1993.

Parnall, Peter. *The Rock*. New York: Macmillan, 1991.

Phillips, K. A. *Common Rocks in Manitoba*. Winnipeg: Natural Resources and Environmental Management, 1975.

Shuttlesworth, Dorothy Edwards. *The Story of Rocks*. Garden City, NY: Doubleday, 1966.

Swenson, Valerie. *A Child's Book of Stones and Minerals*. New York: Maxton Publishers, 1955.

Symes, R.F. *Rocks and Minerals*. Eyewitness Series. London, UK: Dorling Kindersley, 2008.

Young, Ruth. *The Magic Schoolbus Inside the Earth*. Dunedin, FL: Teacher Created Materials, 1995.

Websites

- <http://www.lethsd.ab.ca/lakeview/Classrooms/grade3t/grade3/rocks.htm>

  Rocks and Minerals: This site (designed for grade 3 but with good information for older students) includes extensive links to information on all kinds of rock and mineral formations, as well as picture galleries and links for rock identification and other activities.

- <http://gsc.nrcan.gc.ca/landscapes/index_e.php>

  Geological Survey of Canada (Natural Resources Canada): A collection of photographs of various Canadian landscapes and landforms with brief descriptions and location information.

- <http://www.rocksforkids.com/RFK/howrocks.html>

  How Rocks and Minerals are Formed: This educational site is designed for students in the fourth grade. Includes information on igneous, sedimentary, and metamorphic rocks, Earth, minerals, and a photograph section.

- <http://www.cotf.edu/ete/modules/msese/earthsys.html>

  Earth Floor: Information and activities on Earth cycles, plate tectonics, geological time, and biodiversity.

- <http://www.pep.bc.ca/kids/kids.html>

  Provincial Emergency Program: Features background information and activities on Canada's volcanoes, earthquakes, and other threats. Includes safety tips, games, and links to the Skywatchers' site and other useful sites.

- <http://www.field-trips.org/>

  Tramline Field Trips: Take an extraordinary field trip to anywhere in the world, from salt marshes to deserts to volcanoes, with a professional field guide. Each trip begins with teacher resources and necessary background information, including terms and concepts that are particular to the chosen area. All sites include visuals, legends, and links, and information on plants and animals within the habitat.

- <http://www.chariho.k12.ri.us/curriculum/MISmart/ocean/sand1.htm>

  Sands of the World: This site is an extensive ongoing project initiated by the Chariho Regional School District in Rhode Island. It examines the mineral and sound qualities of beach sand throughout the world. Includes an audio file of booming sand dunes and excellent photo galleries.

- <http://www.ucmp.berkeley.edu//ordovician/winnipeg.html>

  University of California Museum of Paleontology: This article relates to Lake Winnipeg's Alga Flora (fossils of seaweed). Also click on "Home" and type "Learning from the Fossil Records" into the search box for a collection of articles and classroom activities.

- <http://www.ecokids.ca/pub/eco_info/topics/forests/flood_and_erosion.cfm>

  EcoKids: Includes information on deforestation, soil erosion, tree planting, and tree ring analysis, with extensive links to information on climate change and other topics, as well as games and contests.

- <http://www.nrcan.gc.ca/mms/scho-ecol/toc_e.htm>

  Natural Resources Canada's Minerals and Metals: A World to Discover: Start your own mine, find out more about "hidden treasures," and much more.

Introduction

In this unit, students will be introduced to geology. They will examine different types of rocks and minerals, learn about the characteristics and properties of rocks and minerals, and discover their many uses. This unit will also explore how human uses of rocks and minerals not only alter the landscape but have an impact on the environment and on society.

At the beginning of this unit, set up an exploration centre in the classroom where students are free to independently explore rock and mineral collections, and rock identification books. You may wish to encourage family involvement by having students bring items from home that will add to the study of rocks, minerals, and erosion. (Rock and mineral collections can also be obtained through geological societies, local departments of mines and natural resources, as well as through science supply catalogues.)

Collect and display books about rocks, minerals, and erosion in a science or book corner of your classroom. Please see page 198 for suggestions.

Collect pictures from magazines, tourism publications, and calendars of different landscapes in your local community and throughout the world.

If possible, contact local guest speakers from the community to talk to students about subjects relating to rocks, minerals, and erosion. Some interesting topics may include rock collecting, gem formation, earthquakes, and volcanoes.

Science Vocabulary

Continue to use your science and technology word wall to display new vocabulary as it is introduced. Throughout this unit, teachers should use, and encourage students to use, vocabulary such as: *rock, mineral, colour,*
texture, lustre, hardness, crystal, igneous, sedimentary, metamorphic, fossil, environment, landscape, and *landform.*

Materials Required for the Unit

Classroom: coloured pencils or markers, chart paper, felt pens, overhead projector, Plaster of Paris, scissors, white paper, masking tape, chalk, KWL chart, modelling clay (two colours), string, overhead transparency, rulers, glue, mural paper

Book, Pictures, and Illustrations: mineral resource guides books and/or DVDs/videos about volcanoes, a variety of pictures of different landscapes (natural and those that are the result of human activity) from magazines, newspapers, calendars, local tourism brochures, and so on, writings about the mining industry (literature selections, industry publications, newspaper articles, advertisements, promotional material, government publications), magazines and catalogues that show examples of objects made from rock and mineral materials, sample three-point approach chart (included)

Household: paper towels, small mixing bowls, clear plastic cups, empty milk cartons, newspaper, toothbrushes or other small brushes, coffee cans with lids, plastic shopping bags, string, recipe cards, drinking straws, basin or aluminum roasting pan, tweezers, paper plates

Equipment: freezer

Other: collection of rocks, sets of six mineral specimens (one for each group of students), magnifying glasses, hardness kits (penny, streak plate [unglazed tile], steel nail), samples of metamorphic rock, samples of igneous rock, coloured sand, fine blue aquarium gravel, large gravel or pebbles, shells, sedimentary rocks (shale, sandstone, limestone), 1–kg bag of patching cement (found at most hardware stores), 1-L bag of vermiculite (from the garden store or nursery), Popsicle sticks, safety goggles, clay, samples of different products derived from rocks and minerals (e.g., a brick, china, chalk, jewellery, dry wall, talcum powder, coins, soapstone carvings), soft cloths, cookies that contain a variety of ingredients, ice-cream pails, rock and mineral samples from a variety of places, samples (or pictures) of fossils, hard objects (twigs, chicken bones)

A Note About Materials

The materials needed to complete some activities are extensive. Teachers should review the materials lists for the unit ahead of time and make a note of items that students may be able to bring from home (for example, plastic containers, paper plates and/or cups, spoons, pie plates, fabric samples, balls of wool). Then, prior to beginning the lesson, teachers can send a letter home with students asking parents/guardians to donate some of these materials.

A Note About Safety

During their exploration of rocks and minerals, students should be able to identify, and understand, the importance of some fundamental practices that will ensure their safety and the safety of others. This includes knowing that some places are unsafe for collecting rock samples (for example, construction sites). Students should also know that they need to wear protective eyewear when they are conducting investigations such as chipping samples.

1 | Identifying Rocks and Minerals

Expectations

- **2.3** Use a variety of criteria to classify common rocks and minerals according to their characteristics

- **2.5** Use appropriate science and technology vocabulary, including *hardness, colour, lustre,* and *texture,* in oral and written communication

- **2.6** Use a variety of forms to communicate with different audiences and for a variety of purposes

- **3.1** Describe the difference between rocks and minerals, and explain how these differences make them suitable for human use

Science Background Information for Teachers

Rocks are made up of two or more minerals. Granite, for example, is composed of three kinds of minerals: quartz, feldspar, and mica. A mineral is composed of the same substance throughout. Most rocks on Earth are made up of just five kinds of minerals: calcite, quartz, feldspar, mica, and hornblende.

Materials

- KWL chart (made on chart paper, as in example below)

What We Think We Know About Rocks and Minerals	What We Want to Know About Rocks and Minerals	What We Learned About Rocks and Minerals

- cookies that contain a variety of ingredients (e.g., raisins, chocolate chips, nuts)

Note: Make sure none of your students are allergic to any of the ingredients in the cookies, particularly nuts. If you have a student with a nut (or other) allergy, find a substitute ingredient (e.g., cookies with raisins, chocolate chips, or marshmallows).

- paper towels
- tweezers
- collection of rocks
- coloured pencils or markers
- magnifying glasses

Activity

Introduce the unit by challenging students to present what they already know about rocks and minerals. Record their ideas in the first column of the KWL chart.

Focus on the terms *rock* and *mineral*. Explain to students that rocks are made up of two or more minerals. Distribute one cookie to each student. Explain that the cookie represents a rock, and the pieces inside the cookie (raisins, chocolate chips, nuts, and so on) represent minerals, such as gold and silver. Challenge students to be "miners" and remove the "minerals" from the cookies. Have students break their cookies apart and use tweezers to separate the "minerals" into piles.

Now, explain to students that a mineral is made up of only one material. Ask:

- How is your cookie like a rock?
- How are the nuts, chocolate chips, or raisins in your cookie like a mineral?

Divide the class into working groups. Distribute rocks from the exploration centre (see introduction to Unit 4, page 200) to each group, along with magnifying glasses. Have students observe the rocks and discuss their observations with others in their groups.

▶

Ask:

- How would you describe your rocks?
- Are all your rocks the same?
- How are your rocks different?

Have students in each group select one rock from their collection and examine it closely. Ask:

- What colour is the rock?
- Does the rock look the same throughout?
- Can you find any minerals in your rock?

Have each group compare its rock with the rock from another group. Ask:

- Are the rocks the same?
- How are they different?

Following this exploration, have students brainstorm a list of things they would like to learn about rocks and minerals. Record these ideas in the second column of the KWL chart.

Provide students with plenty of time to examine and manipulate rocks and minerals. Encourage them to describe the unique features of each, so that they can begin the process of identifying both rocks and minerals.

Note: Throughout the unit, as students learn new concepts about rocks and minerals, have them complete the third column of the KWL chart.

Activity Sheet A

Directions to students:

Draw a diagram of your cookie "rock." Label the "minerals" in your cookie rock. Now, draw a diagram of one of the real rocks that you examined. Explain the difference between a rock and a mineral (4.1.1).

Activity Centre

Set up a table with rock collections (number the rocks so students can refer to the numbers when examining, describing, and sorting them), rock identification books, minerals, and magnifying glasses. Encourage students to independently explore the rocks and minerals, sort them, and identify them by name. Provide paper, coloured pencils, and markers for students to sketch pictures of the rocks. You may also encourage students to bring rocks from home to add to the classroom collection.

Extensions

- Let students make their own cookie rocks, using ingredients of their choice (chocolate chips, butterscotch chips, marshmallows, nuts).

- Have students research the mining process to determine how minerals are removed from rock.

- Challenge students to start their own rock and mineral collections and to identify their specimens.

Assessment Suggestion

As students work in their groups, observe their abilities to use the terms *rock* and *mineral* and distinguish between the two. Use the Anecdotal Record sheet, found on page 19, to record results.

Rocks and Minerals

Cookie Rock	Real Rock

What is a rock? _____

_____

_____

What is a mineral? _____

_____

_____

Portage & Main Press, 2008, Hands-on Science & Technology, Grade 4, BLM, ISBN: 978-1-55379-179-9

2 | Classifying Rocks and Minerals

Expectations

- **2.1** Follow established safety procedures for outdoor activities and for working with tools, materials, and equipment

- **2.3** Use a variety of criteria to classify common rocks and minerals according to their characteristics

- **2.5** Use appropriate science and technology vocabulary, including *hardness, colour, lustre*, and *texture*, in oral and written communication

- **2.6** Use a variety of forms to communicate with different audiences and for a variety of purposes

- **3.2** Describe the properties that are used to identify minerals

Materials

- plastic shopping bags (doubled) or ice-cream pails (for collecting rocks and minerals)
- string
- rock and mineral samples from a variety of locations (e.g., local environment and other locations)
- chart paper
- markers

Activity: Part One

Note: Select a location where students can collect rock samples. You may wish to talk to a local rock and mineral club to determine the best place to collect rocks and minerals in your community.

Explain to students that you are going to take them on a "rock walk." Divide the class into pairs of students, and provide each pair with a pail or bag for collecting samples. Explain to students that when they return to the classroom they are going to compare and sort their rocks and minerals based on common characteristics. Encourage students to look for a variety of rocks and minerals.

Before leaving on your walk, review the safety rules to observe when exploring outdoor environments. Also, review the importance of respecting the environment. Ask:

- What are some rules you need to remember when exploring outdoor environments? (walk only in designated areas, stay together in a group, keep your eyes open for dangerous items such as poison ivy, watch for loose rocks, ensure safe footing)

- How can you respect the environment during your walk? (be careful not to step on or destroy living things, put things back where you found them, make sure you return all equipment/materials you brought with you on the walk)

When students have returned from their rock walk, brainstorm, as a class, ways that the rocks and minerals can be sorted (for example, by colour, size, shape, texture, and shininess).

Note: Introduce the term *lustre* as a way of describing the shininess of rocks and minerals.

With a partner, have students find a place in the classroom where they can spread out their collections. Ask students in each pair to select a way to sort their rocks and minerals and place a circle of string around each grouping. Once students have sorted their collections, have them team up with another pair and try to identify how the other pair sorted its collection.

Challenge students to sort their collection by more than one attribute.

▶

Once students have had an opportunity to sort their collections in a variety of ways, ask:

■ What are some of the attributes you used to sort and classify your collections?

Record students' responses on chart paper.

Activity: Part Two

Evenly distribute a large selection of rocks and minerals from the class collection (not from those just collected during the previous activty, but from collections used in previous activities). Have students repeat the sorting activity, using these samples, and challenge other student pairs to guess the sorting rules. After students have had several opportunities to sort in different ways, ask:

■ Did you use any different or additional attributes to sort your sample of rocks and minerals?

■ How are the rocks and minerals you collected on your walk similar to rocks collected from other locations?

■ Why do you think these rocks are similar?

■ How are the rocks and minerals you collected on your walk different from rocks and minerals from other locations?

■ Why do you think they are different?

Brainstorm an extensive list of descriptors for the various rocks and minerals. Record these on chart paper. Students can refer to the list when selecting descriptors to Activity Sheet A (4.2.1).

Activity Sheet A

Directions to students:

Select six rocks and minerals from your collection. List five descriptive words across the top of the chart (for example, smooth, rough,

flat, round, dark coloured, light coloured, large, small). Draw a diagram of each of your rocks/minerals in the left-hand column. Use a checkmark to show the descriptive words that describe each rock/mineral (4.2.1).

Activity Centre

Encourage students to sort the rock and mineral collections into groups, based on common attributes. Have students take photographs of their collections once they have been sorted. Display the pictures on a bulletin board so that students can review the various ways to sort materials.

Extensions

■ Have students use a weigh scale to compare the mass of the rocks and minerals. Record the mass of each rock and mineral. Extend this activity by soaking the rocks and minerals in water overnight. Measure and record the mass of the rocks and minerals once again. Compare the masses of the rocks and minerals before and after soaking. See if their masses have changed, and discuss why this occurred.

■ Have students cut and paste (or draw and colour) pictures of rocks and minerals onto index cards. Encourage students to invent games, such as "Rock and Mineral Concentration" (match identical rock and mineral pictures) or "Rock and Mineral Rummy" (group pictures by a common attribute).

Describing Rocks and Minerals

Rock/Mineral	Descriptors				
#1					
#2					
#3					
#4					
#5					
#6					

3 Classifying Minerals

Expectations

- **2.1** Follow established safety procedures for outdoor activities and for working with tools, materials, and equipment

- **2.2** Use a variety of tests to identify the physical properties of minerals

- **2.3** Use a variety of criteria to classify common rocks and minerals according to their characteristics

- **2.5** Use appropriate science and technology vocabulary, including *hardness, colour, lustre*, and *texture*, in oral and written communication

- **2.6** Use a variety of forms to communicate with different audiences and for a variety of purposes

- **3.1** Describe the difference between rocks and minerals, and explain how these differences make them suitable for human use

- **3.2** Describe the properties that are used to identify minerals

Science Background Information for Teachers

The physical properties of minerals can be determined using several specific tests. These tests are used by geologists to identify minerals:

Hardness

- measured on a scale of 1–10
- tested by scratching the mineral with a fingernail, penny, glass, and steel nail (the mineral must be scratched in the order given)
- Mohs' Hardness Scale used to determine hardness

- a magnifying glass used to see the surface more clearly to check for scratches

Streak Colour

Mohs' Hardness Scale 1 (softest) to 10 (hardest)	
Hardness	**Mineral**
1	Talc
2	Gypsum
3	Calcite
4	Flourite
5	Apatite
6	Orthoclase
7	Quartz
8	Topaz
9	Corundum
10	Diamond

- an unglazed tile called a *streak plate* is used
- corner of mineral is rubbed on tile several times to see if it leaves a colour (some streak colours will be different from the colour of the mineral)
- if mineral is harder than the streak plate, it will not leave a streak colour
- a magnifying glass is used to find out the exact colour of the streak

Lustre

- the surface appearance of a mineral is described as *glassy, metallic, dull*, or *shiny*

Texture

- the feel of the surface of a mineral is described as *rough, smooth, soapy*, or *bumpy*

Colour

- the colour of the mineral is described

Note: Some minerals are different colours, e.g., pink and white quartz, while others are always the same colour.

3

Materials

- several sets of 6 mineral specimens, numbered from 1 to 6 (one for each working group of students. Use small pieces of masking tape for labelling specimens)
- magnifying glasses
- hardness kits: each kit should include a penny, a piece of glass (tape the edges of small mirrors or pieces of glass), and a steel nail
- overhead transparency of Activity Sheet A (4.3.1)
- overhead projector
- unglazed tiles
- mineral resource guides

Activity

Divide the class into working groups, and provide each group with a set of six minerals numbered from 1 to 6. Have students examine and compare the minerals. Ask:

- How are the minerals the same?
- How are they different?

Explain to students that minerals have certain properties or characteristics that enable them to identified. On chart paper, record the five properties that will be tested (colour, lustre, texture, streak colour, and hardness). Ask students for suggestions on how each mineral could be tested for each property.

Once you have reviewed each mineral property, provide each group with Activity Sheet A (4.3.1), and use the overhead transparency to review the chart. First, focus on colour. Have students examine mineral sample #1 and describe its colour. Have them record the colour in the appropriate column on their activity sheets. Now, have the groups do the same for each mineral sample, deciding on one colour that best describes each mineral.

Review the term *lustre* as a way of describing the shininess of a mineral. Introduce the four descriptive terms used to describe lustre (*glassy, metallic, dull,* and *shiny*). Have students examine the minerals and select the term that best describes each. Have students record this in the appropriate column on their activity sheet.

Review the term *texture,* and introduce the four descriptors (*rough, smooth, soapy,* and *bumpy*). Have students manipulate the minerals and select the term that best describes each mineral's texture. Have students record this on their activity sheets.

Provide each group with an unglazed tile. Explain that streak colour is determined by rubbing a mineral on the tile to see what colour is left on the tile. Have students test each mineral for streak colour and record the colour left on the tile in the appropriate column on their activity sheets.

Note: If the minerals are harder than the tile, a streak will not be visible. In this case, students should record "no streak" on the chart.

For testing hardness, provide groups with a penny, a piece of glass, and a nail. Have students first test a mineral for hardness by scratching it with a fingernail. Then, have them scratch the minerals with the penny, the glass, and the steel nail, in that order. Have them examine the mineral with a magnifying glass each time to see if a scratch is left on the mineral. On their activity sheets, they can check off each object that left a scratch on the mineral.

Note: Mohs' Hardness Scale will not be used at this stage to test hardness.

Once students have completed their description of the six mineral specimens, challenge them to use a mineral resource guide to identify the minerals.

▶

3

Activity Sheet A

Note: This activity sheet is to be completed during the activity.

Directions to students:

Test the properties of the six mineral specimens. Use a mineral resource guide to help you identify each mineral (4.3.1).

Extensions

- Introduce a simplified version of Mohs' Hardness Scale (below), and have students use this scale to test minerals for hardness.

Mohs' Hardness Scale 1 (softest) to 10 (hardest)	
Minerals scratched by:	**Hardness:**
fingernail	2.5 or less
penny	3 or less
glass	5.5 or less
steel nail	6.5 or less
none of the above	greater than 6.5

- Have students repeat the (above) experiment extension activity, using different minerals.

- Have students develop riddles about different minerals based on identified properties. For example, I am light grey with a little bit of white. I feel smooth, almost like soap. I am dull and can be scratched by a fingernail. What am I? (Answer: talc)

Assessment Suggestions

- Circulate around the classroom, and observe students as they conduct tests on the physical properties of their mineral specimens. Use the Anecdotal Record sheet, found on page 19, to record results.

- As students work in their groups, observe their abilities to work together cooperatively. Use the Cooperative Skills Teacher Assessment sheet, found on page 25, to record results.

- Have students complete a Cooperative Skills Self-Assessment sheet, found on page 27, to reflect on their abilities to work together.

Classifying Minerals

Mineral	Colour	Lustre	Texture	Streak Colour	Hardness	Name of Mineral
#1					fingernail____ penny _____ glass _____ steel nail____	
#2					fingernail____ penny _____ glass _____ steel nail____	
#3					fingernail____ penny _____ glass _____ steel nail____	
#4					fingernail____ penny _____ glass _____ steel nail____	
#5					fingernail____ penny _____ glass _____ steel nail____	
#6					fingernail____ penny _____ glass _____ steel nail____	

Portage & Main Press, 2008, Hands-on Science & Technology, Grade 4, BLM, ISBN: 978-1-55379-179-9

4 Three Classes of Rock

Expectations

- **2.3** Use a variety of criteria to classify common rocks and minerals according to their characteristics

- **2.5** Use appropriate science and technology vocabulary, including *hardness, colour, lustre*, and *texture*, in oral and written communication

- **3.3** Describe how igneous, sedimentary, and metamorphic rocks are formed

- **3.4** Describe the characteristics of the three classes of rocks, and explain how their characteristics are related to their origin

Science Background Information for Teachers

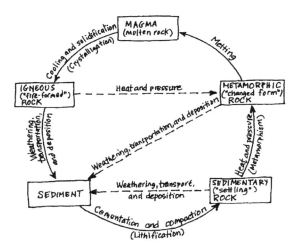

Igneous rock: Molten (melted) rock found kilometres deep under Earth's crust is called *magma*. When magma cools and hardens, either above or below ground level, it is called *igneous rock*. The most common igneous rock is granite. Other examples are the volcanic rocks pumice and obsidian.

Sedimentary rock: Exposed igneous or metamorphic rocks undergo weathering by wind, rain, ice, and so on. The small particles of rock, called *sediment*, eventually settle (usually in horizontal beds) in lakes or oceans. As more sediment is deposited, the layers become compacted, forming sedimentary rock. Some examples of sedimentary rock are sandstone, limestone, and shale. Fossils are often found in sedimentary rock.

Metamorphic rock: Massive pressure and extremely high temperatures involved in mountain building can change the sedimentary rock layers or igneous rock into metamorphic rock. These are formed when large portions of rock and dirt are folded and pressed into each other as a result of the movement of the earth's crust. Examples are marble (from limestone), slate (from shale), and gneiss (from granite).

Materials

Activity: Part One: Igneous Rock

- books and/or DVDs/videos about volcanoes
- overhead transparency of Activity Sheet A (4.4.1) (cross section of a volcano)
- coloured pencils
- samples of igneous rocks

Activity: Part Two: Metamorphic Rock

- 2 different colours of modelling clay
- sheets of paper
- books
- rulers
- samples of metamorphic rock

Activity: Part Three: Sedimentary Rock

- sedimentary rocks (shale, sandstone, limestone)
- newspaper
- coloured sand
- fine, blue aquarium gravel
- large gravel or pebbles
- shells

4

- small mixing bowls
- Plaster of Paris
- clear plastic cups
- empty milk cartons (one for each group)
- sample three-point approach chart (included) (4.4.4)

Activity: Part One: Igneous Rock

Explain to students that rocks are created on Earth in different ways. As a class, read a book or watch a DVD/video that depicts the action of volcanoes. Discuss the book/video/DVD, focusing on magma and lava.

Distribute Activity Sheet A (4.4.1), and have students observe the picture of the volcano. Explain that deep inside Earth is melted rock called *magma*. Tell students that sometimes the magma pushes upward to the surface of Earth. Ask:

- What do you think happens when the magma escapes the volcano?
- What is another name for magma as it escapes the volcano? (lava)
- What happens to the lava when it flows out onto Earth's surface?

Explain to students that as the lava cools it forms into rocks. These rocks are called *igneous rocks*. Igneous rocks are rocks that have been "made by fire" (igneous means "fiery"). Display several samples of igneous rocks for students to manipulate and examine.

Work through the activity sheet together as a class. Ask students, once again:

- What is the melted rock inside Earth called?

Have students colour the magma red. Ask:

- What is the magma called when it reaches the surface of Earth?

Have students colour the lava that flows down the sides of the volcano orange. Ask:

- What happens to the layers of lava after they have flowed down the sides of the volcano?

Have students colour the layers of hardened lava and ash that pile up brown.

Activity Sheet A

Note: Students are to complete this activity sheet during Activity: Part One.

Directions to students:

Colour your diagram of the volcano. Explain how igneous rocks are formed (4.4.1).

Activity: Part Two: Metamorphic Rock

Display samples of metamorphic rock, such as slate and marble. Have students examine and describe the specimens. Explain that some rocks are formed from intense heat or pressure inside the earth.

Provide each student with two colours of modelling clay. Have students use one colour to form a flat strip about 1 centimetre thick, 10 centimetres wide, and 15 centimetres long. Now, have them make 10 small, round balls with the other colour of clay (each about 1 centimetre in diameter), and place the clay balls on the clay strip (see below). Have students draw a diagram of the clay model on Activity Sheet B (4.4.2).

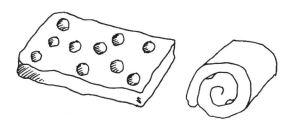

▶

4

Now, have students roll up the clay strip (see second figure on previous page) and draw a diagram of the changed model. Ask:

■ What do you think would happen to your clay model if a lot of force or pressure was placed on it?

Have students test their predictions by placing a piece of paper over the clay, putting a book on top of the paper, and pressing down firmly.

Note: This action represents pressure inside Earth that is forced upon rock matter.

After students carefully remove the book and paper, have them use the edge of a ruler to cut the compressed clay in half. Ask:

■ How has the clay changed?
■ What caused this change?

Discuss the change in form of the clay as a result of the pressure. Have students draw a diagram on Activity Sheet B (4.4.2) to show what the clay looks like now.

Activity Sheet B

Note: Students are to complete this activity sheet during Activity: Part Two.

Directions to students:

Draw diagrams of the changes in your clay model. Now, explain how metamorphic rocks are formed (4.4.2).

Activity: Part Three: Sedimentary Rocks

Explain to students that they are going to study the third type of rock form, called *sedimentary rock*. Pass around the samples of shale, sandstone, and limestone for students to observe. Ask students:

■ How would you describe sedimentary rocks?
■ What do sedimentary rocks look like?

■ How do you think sedimentary rocks are formed?

Tell students that they are going to make their own models of sedimentary rock. Divide the class into working groups. Have the groups cover their workspace with newspaper. Prepare the Plaster of Paris, and pour it into the empty milk cartons.

Note: Plaster will begin to set relatively quickly, so it must be used immediately to build the models.

Give each group a carton of Plaster of Paris and a plastic cup. Have students construct their own models of sedimentary rock in a clear plastic cup. Explain to students that they need to alternate layers of dry materials and Plaster of Paris. For example, pour a layer of aquarium gravel into the cup, followed by a layer of plaster. Then add more layers of shells, plaster, gravel, plaster, pebbles, and plaster. Allow students to be creative in constructing their models.

Allow the model "rocks" to harden overnight. The next day, have students break away the cups from the hardened layers. Ask:

■ Which materials in your sedimentary rock can you see?
■ Which materials are hidden?
■ How is your model like the sedimentary rocks that you examined?
■ How is sedimentary rock formed?

Activity Sheet C

Note: Students are to complete this activity sheet during Activity: Part Three.

Directions to students:

Draw and label a diagram of your model sedimentary rock. Describe how you made your model. Now, explain how sedimentary rock is formed (4.4.3).

Activity: Part Four

As a follow-up to studying the three classes of rocks, have groups of students create three-point approach charts to communicate their understanding of how these rocks are formed. This graphic organizer allows students to record a definition, examples, and a diagram of a concept or word. In this case, have students complete charts for igneous rocks, metamorphic rocks, and sedimentary rocks. A sample three-point approach chart (4.4.4) is included on page 219. Students can use copies of this chart or make large charts on chart paper. Have students share their charts with the class.

Extensions

- Have students research famous volcanoes around the world, such as Mount St. Helen.

- Have students build models of the cross section of a volcano and use their model to explain how igneous rocks are formed.

- Research locations where active volcanoes exist, such as the Hawaiian Islands and Iceland, and find out how people deal with the threat of volcanic eruptions.

- Display students' activity sheet diagrams, and have students compare the differences between each model.

- Take students to a local quarry to observe, firsthand, layers of sedimentary rock. Have students draw diagrams of the rock.

- Examine pictures of the Grand Canyon and other landforms that are made up of sedimentary rock.

Assessment Suggestion

Provide various samples of the three types of rocks. During an individual conference, have the student name and sort the rock samples according to type. Also, encourage the student to explain, in his or her own words, how each class of rock is formed. Use the Individual Student Observations sheet, found on page 20, to record results.

Igneous Rock

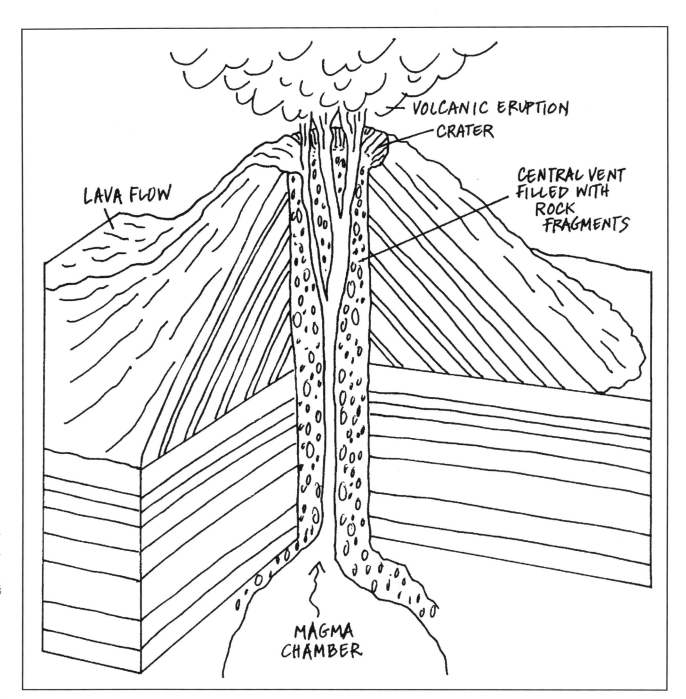

LAVA FLOW

VOLCANIC ERUPTION

CRATER

CENTRAL VENT
FILLED WITH
ROCK
FRAGMENTS

MAGMA
CHAMBER

How are igneous rocks formed? _____

_____

_____

Portage & Main Press, 2008, Hands-on Science & Technology, Grade 4, BLM, ISBN: 978-1-55379-179-9

Metamorphic Rock

Diagrams of My Clay Model

Flat Model

Rolled Model

Cut Model

How are metamorphic rocks formed? _____

_____

_____

Portage & Main Press, 2008, Hands-on Science & Technology, Grade 4, BLM, ISBN: 978-1-55379-179-9

Sedimentary Rock

Sedimentary Rock Model	
Diagram	**How I Made My Model**

How are sedimentary rocks formed? _____

_____

_____

_____

Portage & Main Press, 2008, Hands-on Science & Technology, Grade 4, BLM, ISBN: 978-1-55379-179-9

4C

Three-Point Approach Chart

Definition	Class of Rock	Diagram

Examples

Portage & Main Press, 2008, Hands-on Science & Technology, Grade 4, BLM, ISBN: 978-1-55379-179-9

5 | Fossils

Expectations

- **2.1** Follow established safety procedures for outdoor activities and for working with tools, materials, and equipment

- **2.5** Use appropriate science and technology vocabulary, including *hardness, colour, lustre*, and *texture*, in oral and written communication

- **2.6** Use a variety of forms to communicate with different audiences and for a variety of purposes

- **3.4** Describe the characteristics of the three classes of rocks, and explain how their characteristics are related to their origin

Materials

- samples of fossils or pictures of fossils
- newspaper
- 1-kg bag of patching cement (found at hardware stores)
- 1-L bag of vermiculite (from the garden store or nursery)
- paper plates
- hard objects (e.g., twigs, shells, chicken bones)
- Popsicle sticks
- toothbrushes or other small brushes
- safety goggles
- water
- digital camera
- soft cloth
- reference material about fossils

Activity: Part One

Display samples of fossils or pictures of fossils for students to examine. Ask:

- What are these called?
- What is a fossil?
- How are fossils formed?

- When do you think fossils were formed? (millions of years ago)
- Does the fossil look like something you could find today?
- Why is the study of fossils important?

Explain that fossils are the remains of animals and plants that have become hardened into rocks, or imprints or impressions of plants or animals. Fossils are found in sedimentary rock. As sedimentary rock slowly forms in layers over millions of years, skeletons of animals and the remains of plants get trapped in one of the many layers and create fossils.

Have students examine samples of fossils and determine whether the fossils are the mineralized remains or imprints and impressions of a plant or animal.

Have students cover their desks with newspaper, then have them mix one part dry patching cement to two parts vermiculite. Add water until the mixture resembles dough (the wetter it is, the longer it will take to dry). Have students pour some of this mixture onto paper plates, then press a bone, a seashell, or a twig into the mixture. Tell students to fill the plate with cement mixture, and let it sit until it dries (approximately three days).

Introduce the word *paleontologist*. Explain that a paleontologist is someone who looks for and studies fossils. Have students pretend to be paleontologists. Discuss the procedures they are to follow when they break apart their fossil rocks (for example, wear safety goggles, place a cloth over the rock when chipping, work slowly and carefully, use a soft brush to clean off the fossil). Have students find their hidden fossils.

Activity: Part Two

Plan a field trip to a location where fossils are evident. This may include a visit to a quarry or to a local museum that has fossil specimens. While

5

there, ave students go on a fossil hunt. They can use Activity Sheet A (4.5.1) to keep track of information they gather as they examine fossils.

Note: Take several digital photos of the various fossil specimens for use in Activity: Part Three.

Activity Sheet A

Directions to students:

Draw a diagram of each fossil you find. Describe the object that you think created the fossil (4.5.1).

Activity: Part Three

Following the field trip, have students review their activity sheets, and display the photos of the fossils from the field trip. Have students match their diagrams to the photos.

Have students use the reference material to confirm the identity of the fossils they found on their field trip. Distribute Activity Sheet B (4.5.2) to students, and have them record their research notes on the sheet.

Activity Sheet B

Directions to students:

Research the fossil samples you found on the field trip. In the spaces provided, record your research as jot notes (4.5.2).

Extensions

- Have students use geology books to help them identify plants, animals, or objects that may have created the fossils they found on their fossil hunt.

- Soak sedimentary rock in an open jar of vinegar to dissolve the limestone. Examine the fossils that are released.

Fossil Hunt

Fossil A	Fossil B
I think this fossil was made by a _____.	I think this fossil was made by a _____.
Fossil C	**Fossil D**
I think this fossil was made by a _____.	I think this fossil was made by a _____.
Fossil E	**Fossil F**
I think this fossil was made by a _____.	I think this fossil was made by a _____.

Portage & Main Press, 2008, Hands-on Science & Technology, Grade 4, BLM, ISBN: 978-1-55379-179-9

5A

Researching Fossils

Fossil A	Fossil B
• _____ • _____ • _____ • _____	• _____ • _____ • _____ • _____
Fossil C	**Fossil D**
• _____ • _____ • _____ • _____	• _____ • _____ • _____ • _____
Fossil E	**Fossil F**
• _____ • _____ • _____ • _____	• _____ • _____ • _____ • _____

Portage & Main Press, 2008, Hands-on Science & Technology, Grade 4, BLM, ISBN: 978-1-55379-179-9

6 Identifying the Many Uses of Rocks and Minerals

Expectations

- **2.4** Use scientific inquiry/research skills to investigate how rocks and minerals are used and disposed of in everyday life

Materials

- samples of different products derived from rocks and minerals (e.g., brick, china, chalk, jewellery, dry wall, talcum powder, coins, soapstone carvings)
- magazines and catalogues that show pictures of objects made from rock and mineral materials (hardware catalogues, jewellery flyers, building and architectural magazines, and gardening magazines are good sources for these pictures)
- scissors
- glue
- mural paper

Activity

Have students form a circle in the centre of the classroom. Display the products derived from rocks and minerals in the centre of the circle. Ask students:

- Do you know what all of these products have in common?

Explain that all of the products are derived from rocks and minerals. Hold up one product. Ask:

- What is this product?
- For what is it used?
- From what type of rock or mineral do you think it comes?

Discuss how the properties of rocks and minerals determine what the rocks and minerals are used for. Have students examine a soapstone carving.

Ask:

- Why do you think this is called *soapstone*?
- Do you think soapstone is hard or soft?
- What do you think the results of a scratch test would be on soapstone?

Have students scratch the bottom of the soapstone with their fingernails to determine its softness. Ask:

- Is soapstone soft or hard?
- Why do you think carvings are made from soapstone?
- Would granite be easy to carve?
- Do you think soapstone would be a good material for a building? Why not?

Have students locate pictures of objects made from rock and mineral materials in magazines and catalogues. They can also draw pictures of these items. Create a class mural of all the pictures found that depict objects made from rocks and minerals.

Activity Sheet A

Note: This activity sheet is to completed during Activity: Part One.

Directions to students:

List examples of objects made from rock and mineral materials, and identify what each object is made from (4.6.1).

Activity: Part Two

Take students on a "rock walk" in your community. Have them identify as many rocks and rock products as possible on their walk and record the names on Activity Sheet B (4.6.2).

6

Activity Sheet B

Note: This activity sheet is to be completed during Activity: Part Two.

Directions to students:

Find 10 products in your neighbourhood that are made from rock or minerals. List the products in the spaces provided, and draw an illustration of one of them (4.6.2)

Activity: Part Three

Have students conduct research on products derived from rocks and minerals. Have them complete Activity Sheet C (4.6.3). Once all students have finished their research, bind the pages together in a book about the many uses of rocks and minerals. Display the book in the classroom or school library.

Next, have students research rocks and minerals found in other countries, as well as the products manufactured from them.

Activity Sheet C

Note: This activity sheet is to be completed during Activity: Part Three.

Directions to students:

Select one rock or mineral product, research it, draw a diagram of it, and complete the sentences (4.6.3).

Activity Centre

Have students bring products from home that are derived from rocks and minerals. Display the products on a table at the activity centre. Have students try to guess from which type of rocks and minerals each product is derived.

Objects Made from Rocks and Minerals

Object	Rock/Mineral Material

Portage & Main Press, 2008, Hands-on Science & Technology, Grade 4, BLM, ISBN: 978-1-55379-179-9

Rock/Mineral Products in My Neighbourhood

Ten rock and/or mineral products found in my neighbourhood are:

_____   _____

_____   _____

_____   _____

_____   _____

_____   _____

Portage & Main Press, 2008, Hands-on Science & Technology, Grade 4, BLM, ISBN: 978-1-55379-179-9

Products Derived from Rocks and Minerals

This product is derived from _____

_____

_____

You usually use this product for _____

_____

_____

You can find the product _____

_____

_____

Portage & Main Press, 2008, Hands-on Science & Technology, Grade 4, BLM, ISBN: 978-1-55379-179-9

4C

7 Human Impacts on Habitats and Communities

Expectations

- **1.1** Assess the social and environmental costs and benefits of using objects in the built environment that are made from rocks and minerals

- **1.2** Analyze the impact on society and the environment of extracting and refining rocks and minerals for human use, taking different perspectives into account

- **2.5** Use appropriate science and technology vocabulary, including *hardness, colour, lustre,* and *texture,* in oral and written communication

- **2.6** Use a variety of forms to communicate with different audiences and for a variety of purposes

Note: When students are assessing human impacts on habitats and communities, encourage them to consider a variety of viewpoints. Thoughtful consideration of various viewpoints, as well as the scientific evidence of the environmental costs and risks, will enable students to (1) look for ways in which people might come to agreement on how to minimize the negative impacts of their actions, and (2) make more informed decisions about the choices they make.

Materials

- advertisements relating to the mining industry
- promotional materials relating to the mining industry
- government publications (from Ministry of Natural Resources)
- newspaper items/articles relating to the mining industry
- books (e.g., nonfiction books, stories, novels)
- industry publications
- chart paper
- marker

Activity: Part One

Read aloud from several sources about the benefits mining brings to a town/city/region. Tell students to listen carefully as you read aloud the passages, because you want them to identify the key messages in each. Ask:

- What are the key messages?
- How are the key messages alike?
- How are the key messages different?
- Why are the emphasis and information provided in each source different?

Divide the class into student pairs, and have students use the procedure "think, pair, share" to encourage additional discussion of the topic.

Next, as a class, summarize the key messages and issues presented in the various resources, as well as any questions that students may have about them. On chart paper, make a chart (see below), and record students' responses.

Source	Key Messages	Issues/Questions

Activity: Part Two

Have students select reading/graphic materials from the resources you have provided. Give students plenty of time to read (from two or three sources) the information, independently or with a partner.

Note: Depending on the reading level of your students and the availability of time, you may choose to have the whole class read the same articles and create anchor charts of key ideas. This approach allows you to focus instruction on content-area reading skills.

▶

7

Distribute a copy of Activity Sheet A (4.7.1) to each student. Have students record their findings on the activity sheets after they read each item. When all students have completed their readings and recorded their findings, have each student (or student pair) pass his/her reading materials to the student (student pair) to his/her right. Repeat this process until students have read and commented on a number of different resources.

Next, as a class, discuss students' findings and interpretations. Add all the key messages, issues, and questions that students identified to the anchor chart created in Activity: Part One.

Note: For this activity to be effective, it is important for several students to read and comment on the same materials.

Activity: Part Three

Read aloud the following:

Clay has been discovered in Town *X*, and a mine is about to be developed there. Many people in town support the mine. Clay is used to make plates and mugs, bricks for buildings, and things like kitty litter. However, many townspeople are against the mine, because clay is strip mined, and the products made from it are persistent in the environment.

In pairs or small groups, have students discuss the pros and cons of building the mine. Have students consider the point of view and opinions of the following people:

■ town mayor
■ mining company president
■ owner of the land
■ person who will work in the mine
■ bank president
■ local school principal
■ store owner
■ environmentalist
■ farmer

Alternatively, as a class, create scenarios and roles for an impromptu "in-role" discussion.

Following the discussion(s), ask students:

■ Why were there so many different responses, opinions, and interpretations?
■ What issues came up that are not on the chart (from Activity: Part One/Two)?

Extension

Have students write a persuasive paragraph about why or why not oil drilling should be permitted in areas where habitats could be affected.

Mining Perspectives

Source	Key Message	Issues/Questions

Portage & Main Press, 2008, Hands-on Science & Technology, Grade 4, BLM, ISBN: 978-1-55379-179-9

References for Teachers

Friedl, Alfred. *Teaching Science to Children: An Inquiry Approach*. Toronto: McGraw-Hill College Division, 1996.

Levenson, Elaine. *Teaching Children About Life and Earth Sciences: Activities Every Teacher and Parent Can Use*. New York: McGraw-Hill, 1994.

_____. *Teaching Children About Science*. New York: Tab Books, 1994.

Ricciuti, Edward R., and Margaret W. Carruthers. *National Audubon Society First Field Guide: Rocks and Minerals*. New York: Scholastic, 1998.

Ticotsky, Alan. *Who Says You Can't Teach Science?* Tucson, AZ: Good Year Books, 2004.